New Directions for Adult and Continuing Education

Susan Imel
Jovita M. Ross-Gordon
COEDITORS-IN-CHIEF

I1027599

The Struggle for Democracy in Adult Education

Dianne Ramdeholl
Tania Giordani
Thomas Heaney
Wendy Yanow
EDITORS

Number 128 • Winter 2010
Jossey-Bass
San Francisco

THE STRUGGLE FOR DEMOCRACY IN ADULT EDUCATION
Dianne Ramdeholl, Tania Giordani, Thomas Heaney, Wendy Yanow (eds.)
New Directions for Adult and Continuing Education, no. 128
Susan Imel, Jovita M. Ross-Gordon, Coeditors-in-Chief

Microfilm copies of issues and articles are available in 16mm and 35mm, as well as microfiche in 105mm, through University Microfilms Inc., 300 North Zeeb Road, Ann Arbor, Michigan 48106-1346.

NEW DIRECTIONS FOR ADULT AND CONTINUING EDUCATION (ISSN 1052-2891, electronic ISSN 1536-0717) is part of The Jossey-Bass Higher and Adult Education Series and is published quarterly by Wiley Subscription Services, Inc., A Wiley Company, at Jossey-Bass, 989 Market Street, San Francisco, California 94103-1741. Periodicals Postage Paid at San Francisco, California, and at additional mailing offices. POSTMASTER: Send address changes to New Directions for Adult and Continuing Education, Jossey-Bass, 989 Market Street, San Francisco, California 94103-1741.

New Directions for Adult and Continuing Education is indexed in CIJE: Current Index to Journals in Education (ERIC); Contents Pages in Education (T&F); ERIC Database (Education Resources Information Center); Higher Education Abstracts (Claremont Graduate University); and Sociological Abstracts (CSA/CIG).

SUBSCRIPTIONS for print and electronic in the U.S. cost $98.00 for individuals and $298.00 for institutions, agencies, and libraries.

EDITORIAL CORRESPONDENCE should be sent to the Coeditors-in-Chief, Susan Imel, ERIC/ACVE, 1900 Kenny Road, Columbus, Ohio 43210-1090, e-mail: imel.l@osu.edu; or Jovita M. Ross-Gordon, Southwest Texas State University, EAPS Dept., 601 University Drive, San Marcos, TX 78666.

Cover photograph by Jack Hollingsworth@Photodisc

www.josseybass.com

CONTENTS

EDITORS' NOTES

Most citizens resist unwarranted controls over their day-to-day lives and value the ability to negotiate their own paths. In this, they can be said to favor a democratic practice in which they have a voice at the planning table when decisions are made that affect them. But as we have seen, many want more. In pursuit of their own interests there are those who seek to control others. In the quest for power and domination, democracy fades into a ghostly shade. Recent debates over national health care in the United States, riddled as they have been with misinformation and distortion, demonstrate both the need for grounded knowledge and the will to resolve complex issues—both essential to democratic decision making. Democracy yields, however, to overpowering self-interest. In the face of globalization and massive institutional power, there continues to be a critical role for adult educators to inform and inspire the practice of democracy.

History is as much a tale of what could have been as it is the story of what "really" happened. The history of adult education is a recent story, a short history of promises—some kept and many broken. There is a major contradiction at the core of adult education history in the United States—a polar tension between education for the building of democracy and education for the production of capital.

Adult education in the United States began with democracy. Early in the twentieth century, many began describing adult education as a "movement," a spontaneous emergence of study circles, town hall meetings, and learning groups—all engaged in better understanding their world to collectively build a better one—democratically. Education in its broadest sense—learning to name the world—was at the center of that movement.

At the same time, and at the opposite end of the spectrum, were those who made the leap from lifelong learning to lifelong schooling. Collapse of the almost-movement was inevitable. Educators in the workplace and in formal institutions of learning sought to shape minds, rather than free them. As a result a democratizing adult education grew up alongside a practice that devalued learning for democratic action and stressed adaptation to the workplace, corporate America, and a consumer economy.

Perhaps nostalgia is a lingering desire to return to a past that never was but many adult educators, including the authors represented in this book, have been attempting to reclaim their birthright—a critical but steadfast commitment to building democracy. In the following chapters we build on the historic relationship between adult education and democracy. We examine an adult education practice that not only shapes minds, but also seeks to build communities of collaborative action. We explore best practices in shared and informed decision making within different contexts of adult

NEW DIRECTIONS FOR ADULT AND CONTINUING EDUCATION, no. 128, Winter 2010 © 2010 Wiley Periodicals, Inc.
Published online in Wiley Online Library (wileyonlinelibrary.com) • DOI: 10.1002/ace.385

education—in the community, the classroom and the university—by focusing on various aspects of our work as adult education practitioners.

Contributors to this volume provide salient examples of democratic practice in different areas of adult education and look critically at the strengths and challenges these examples present. They also relate these best practices to the broader efforts within the adult education field to create shared decision making, bringing stakeholders in the process, both learners and their teachers, to the planning table.

In the first chapter, Stephen Brookfield uses Habermas, Albert, and others to discuss the various dimensions of leading democratically. Brookfield begins the chapter by sharing his definition of democracy and the core elements of the democratic process. Continuing his discussion, Brookfield looks at two concepts that underlie the practice of leading democratically, explains how individuals and society learn this style of leadership, and concludes with a discussion on the perils and pitfalls of leading democratically.

One adult education venue in which democratic action is explicitly a goal is popular education. In Chapter two, Janise Hurtig and Hal Adams reflect on an educational practice in which poor and disenfranchised people take control of their day-to-day lives in dialogue with each other. They discuss the formation of small writing groups as a microcosm reflecting a wider and more far-reaching democratic society.

In Chapter three, Dianne Ramdeholl and John Gordon document the history of the Open Book, a New York-based adult literacy program in which staff and students strove to create an egalitarian community and implement authentic student participation in decision making. Using oral histories of participants, the authors explore the significance of the Open Book program by looking at the role it played in creating a sense of hope and possibility and analyzing the extent to which the program made contributions to larger social movements. The authors conclude by showing how the narratives in their study can support other programs struggling to ground their practice in liberatory paradigms.

In Chapter four, Mechthild Hart describes how immigrant domestic workers in metro Chicago have learned to move against the grain of the multiple interlocking social norms associated with "women's work." When an entire working population is being erased from the mainstream, it is tremendously challenging for the workers to find their own voice, claim a democratic space, and form alliances with others to engage in effective collective action.

In Chapter five, Paul Jurmo continues the exploration of work-related education by addressing issues of participatory democracy and decision making as they relate to the workplace. In particular, he explores the role of adult educators in facilitating the participation of workers in decisions that directly affect them such as health, safety, and productivity.

Much adult education takes place in colleges and universities, yet institutions of higher learning are frequently perceived as bastions of the elite and guardians of privileged knowledge. We ask in this volume whether there is space within these tradition-bound institutions for a democratic practice. In Chapter six, Dianne Ramdeholl, Tania Giordani, Tom Heaney, and Wendy Yanow reflect on their experience in a doctoral program that incorporated at its core a process of governance involving both students and faculty. These authors, three recent graduates, and one faculty member, reflect on their struggles in the academy and in the absence of democratic models in day-to-day life. Interlaced into these struggles was the underlying and frequently unstated issue of race.

In Chapter seven, Tom Heaney expands the discussion beyond the classroom to encompass the college or university as a whole. He questions whether stewardship and the discipline of an institution of higher learning can be guided and maintained when all its stakeholders have voice in decision making. This chapter builds on an affirmative inquiry into colleges and universities committed to shared governance, and identifies dispositions and structures that bring all stakeholders to the planning table, thus democratizing higher education. Using data and evidence gathered from three universities and one community college, the author discusses dispositions and structures capable of sustaining a democratic practice in the academy.

Arthur Wilson and Ronald Cervero have navigated the thorny issues of planning for over a decade. In Chapter eight, they refocus that work on the democratic ethos central to planning practice. Building on a theoretical and practical understanding of politics at the planning table, they provide examples from their own work as academic administrators of ways they have or have not incorporated democratic practices into their decision making.

In the final chapter, Wendy Yanow exposes the ambiguities and complexities of the search for democracy described in this volume. Democracy is proclaimed as a national value without understanding the way the term is compromised in practice by capitalism, racism, and free-market economics. She calls on adult educators to continue the struggle to both understand and to create democratic action.

We, the coeditors, would like to conclude by saying that we recognize that there is a vast range in understanding what constitutes democratic practice: From more familiar models of entering polling booths every four years to less common models where specific structures such as town hall meetings, various committees, and variations of consensus type models of decision making are implemented to ensure multiple access points for people's voices to be heard and prevail in decision making.

A book on democratic practice in adult education seems especially relevant at this moment in time with the country poised for change. There exists at these crossroads in history the potential for change if we the people fight to preserve those spaces. It is in these sites of resistance that possibility can be born, nurtured, and grown to bear fruit. As Maxine Greene (personal communication, December 8, 2003) says, in envisioning a more democratic world, "we must focus on collective dialogue rooted in alternative visions, the possibility between freedom and imagination—the ability to make present what is absent, to summon up a condition that is not yet."

Dianne Ramdeholl
Tania Giordani
Thomas Heaney
Wendy Yanow
Editors

DIANNE RAMDEHOLL is an assistant professor in educational studies at the Harry Van Arsdale Center for Labor Studies, Empire State College, New York.

TANIA GIORDANI is a professor of adult education at the College of Lake County, Grayslake, IL.

THOMAS HEANEY is an associate professor and director of the Adult Education Doctoral Program at National-Louis University, Chicago.

WENDY B. YANOW is adjunct faculty at DePaul University, School for New Learning, Chicago and National-Louis University, College of Arts and Sciences, Chicago, and a consultant in adult education.

New Directions for Adult and Continuing Education • DOI: 10.1002/ace

1

Leading democratically means viewing leadership as a process and function, not a positional responsibility. It involves trusting the extraordinary knowledge of ordinary people and working to ensure that those affected by decisions have the most powerful voices in those decisions and have access to all relevant knowledge.

Leading Democratically

Stephen Brookfield

Democracy is the most venerated of American ideas, the one for which wars are fought and people die. So most people would probably agree that leaders should be able to lead well in a democratic society. Yet, genuinely democratic leadership is a relative rarity. Why is this the case? At root it boils down to an unwillingness—on both the left and the right—to trust people to know what's best for them. On the left is the view that the majority of people live in false consciousness as dupes of capitalism, patriarchy, and White supremacy, and that consequently the needs they mistakenly feel as their own are in fact implanted in them by dominant ideology. On the right is the view that the masses are less intelligent than the elites, regularly exercise poor judgment, and that they must either pay the consequences for their poor choices, or forgo the right to make those choices when they are regarded as immoral (for example, to have an abortion or to marry a same-sex partner). Put this lack of trust in ordinary people in the context of a political system dominated by corporate interests, global capitalism, heightened surveillance, and the deliberate suppression of dissent, and you have a situation in which expecting much democracy is clearly naïve.

Defining democracy is not an easy task, but it is one I need to address. For me, a democratic system exhibits three core elements. First, its members engage in a continuous, ever-widening conversation about how to organize social, economic, and political affairs. To be democratic this conversation must be as inclusive and wide-ranging as possible involving widely different groups and perspectives. It must also be educational in that people are able to make decisions based on full knowledge of the situations in which they find themselves, full awareness of the range of different possible courses of action, and the best information about the potential consequences

NEW DIRECTIONS FOR ADULT AND CONTINUING EDUCATION, no. 128, Winter 2010 © 2010 Wiley Periodicals, Inc.
Published online in Wiley Online Library (wileyonlinelibrary.com) • DOI: 10.1002/ace.386

of their decisions. In Habermas's (1996) terms, democratic action is best facilitated by an ideal speech situation that allows all participants full access to all relevant knowledge pertaining to the issues discussed. Mezirow (1990) used this element of Habermas' work to develop his theory of transformative learning, and it informs his conviction that adult educators need to ally themselves with social movements that seek to secure people's full access to the knowledge that affects how they might live.

A democratic decision draws its legitimacy from the fact that all fully informed stakeholders have been involved in the conversation leading to it. How that decision is arrived varies according to who has the greatest stake in it. This is the argument of Albert's (2004, 2006) work on participatory economics or parecon. In parecon the chief decision makers involved in a conversation are those most affected by that decision. Leading democratically according to this notion focuses on creating conversational forms that are as inclusive as possible and fighting any vested interests concerned to block access to relevant information. When an organization or structure seeks to privatize knowledge and keep it the province of professionals this also inspires adult educators to fight to make this democratically available. Such was the raison d'être of much of John Ohliger's work (Grace and Rocco, 2009).

Second, democracy is an economic arrangement. Democracy is not just a political form involving voting procedures and structures of representation, but an economic one requiring the abolition of vast disparities in wealth, the equalization of income, and the placing of all forms of resources under common control. This is why democracy and socialism are intertwined. Important elements of democracy include many of the things that Franklin D. Roosevelt called for in his 1944 State of the Union Address, sometimes called the Second Bill of Rights (Sunstein, 2006). These include the right to good education, a decent job and livable wage, adequate food and clothing, acceptable medical care, and some protection from the ravages of old age. A socialist economy in which the populace as a whole controls the production and distribution of goods and services (as against control by an unrepresentative, privileged elite) is the most democratic economic arrangement possible.

In adult education one of the best articulations of this idea is W.E.B. Du Bois's "Basic American Negro Creed" (Du Bois, 1971) that was part of a work commissioned by an offshoot of the American Association for Adult Education and then not published (Guy and Brookfield, 2009). Leading according to this notion of democracy entails working to further the interests of organizations, groups, and movements that are trying to establish cooperative economic forms. Du Bois's creed linked the advancement of African Americans and the abolition of racism to socialism. The sixth element of his creed states baldly, "We believe in the ultimate triumph of some form of Socialism the world over; that is, common ownership and control of the means of production and equality of income" (p. 321). This equalizing of work and wealth is urged as "the beginning of the rise of the Negro race in this land and the world over, in power, learning, and accomplishment" (p. 321). This equalization is to be achieved through taxation and through "vesting the ultimate power of the state in the hands of the workers" (p. 321), a situation that will be accompanied by the working class demanding their "proportionate share in administration and public expenditure" (p. 322). Du Bois ends the creed with an expansive appeal to people of all races to join in fighting White supremacy and creating Socialism. In his words "to this vision of work, organization, and service, we welcome men (sic) of all colors so long as their basic subscription to this basic creed is sincere and proven by their deeds" (p. 322).

The third element of my understanding of democracy is that it is a struggle against ideologies that exclude disenfranchised groups from full and equal participation in social life. These ideologies would be those of White supremacy, class superiority, patriarchy, homophobia, ableism, and so on. Western industrial societies purport to be completely open democracies in which all have equal opportunity to flourish, yet they are actually highly unequal societies in which economic inequity, racism, and class discrimination are empirical realities. The way this state of affairs is reproduced as seeming to be normal, natural, and inevitable (thereby heading off potential challenges to the system) is through the dissemination of dominant ideologies. For me democracy can only flourish if these ideologies are challenged and then replaced. From this third perspective, leadership involves subverting and destroying elements of dominant ideology.

From a leadership perspective, leading democratically views leadership as a function or process, rather than as an individual, or group of individuals', exercise of certain behaviors. The process of democratic leadership includes two specific, indispensable, and inseparable notions. First, everyone potentially has a responsibility to lead, to put their energies and talents at the service of the group, and to be held accountable for their actions to the group. Although who is exercising leadership varies according to the specific tasks involved and the need for specific skills or knowledge that only some possess, all involved are required to assist and support the temporary leader and also to help decide when temporary leadership should change.

Second, everyone has a right to lead—to participate fully and have an equal opportunity to influence the outcome of deliberations regarding how we are to share resources and ensure all have equal life chances. Without faith in the ultimate ability of everyone to exercise leadership, democracy cannot last. Without avenues for everyone's voice to be heard, democracy withers. Leaders committed to a genuine democracy do not hesitate to lament publicly how grievously people's talents have been wasted in the past. They do this not to make trouble or to accentuate the negative, but to bring attention to the way that the everyday wisdom of extraordinary people has historically been so often underutilized. Most of all, they study the destructive and exclusionary patterns of the past closely to avoid repeating them in the present and to emphasize how much richer our society would be if everyone's capacity for leadership were fully developed.

Learning to Lead Democratically

The animating metaphor for democracy is dialogue—people in constant and meaningful communication with each other. Through dialogue people learn to listen as well as speak, to learn as well as teach, to follow as well as lead, to collaborate more readily than to labor in solitude. The democratic dialogue supports a shared existence that is responsive to each community member's voiced needs and concerns. As with any good dialogue, time is set aside to pose questions, to prioritize issues, and to solve problems. Dialogue helps us know our neighbors better and learn how to create, out of the disparate elements of any diverse community, a workable consensus. Dialogue also helps us become more than an individual with private interests. In its give and take we learn how to be members of a public group looking after our shared interests.

Democratic faith rests on the idea that ordinary people are more likely than isolated elites or narrowly trained experts to make decisions that are in the broad interests of the majority of people. In Mary Parker Follett's (1924) terms, expert knowledge must always be democratized, its application guided by the working majority. Democratic power is power that is broadly distributed to serve the common good. An important dimension of this shared power is the community knowing its members well enough to understand how they can serve and lead from their strengths as empowered members of the community. This is the approach that the Industrial Areas Foundations (<http://www.industrialareasfoundation.org/>) has taken for many years. Democracy for the IAF, established by Chicago organizer Saul Alinsky some 65 years ago, begins with relationship building. Through relationships, both private and public, IAF builds its democratic base and learns how each individual participant can contribute her or his distinct strengths to the promotion of a shared and common good. For Ed Chambers, IAF's current executive director, there is nothing inherently sinister about power. It can be employed for good or ill. It can be practiced in a limited, one way, unilateral manner, or it can be as unlimited and reciprocal as any set of meaningful relationships. Power—collectively and authentically exercised— is, after all, the basis of empowerment.

Learning to lead democratically in the cause of empowerment entails learning to distinguish each distinctive voice in the sometimes overwhelming cacophony of democratic deliberations. Who each community member is, what each person most needs, how each individual can best contribute to the group's well-being, are all concerns that democratic leaders—which means, potentially, everyone—must learn to address. As James Baldwin noted in the opening pages of *Notes of a Native Son* (1955) leaders can easily lose

New Directions for Adult and Continuing Education • DOI: 10.1002/ace

sight of the individual, glossing over rich differences and astounding distinctiveness, in their haste to draw the sort of generalizations that shape social policy. For Baldwin, this meant there was much danger in attempting to draw any meaningful and valid conclusions about the "Black Experience." For a Native American leader, who is keenly aware of the 500 plus highly diverse tribes that are federally recognized, reaching useful generalizations about the American Indian would seem a perilous exercise indeed.

Generalizations about racial group membership or cultural identity, though well meaning, discount how people specifically and concretely relate to each other and form communities together. They omit all the gritty, messy details of individual lives. The strength of democracy lies in these details, particularly in the mix of different traditions, cultures, and languages. Democratic leaders view these as strengths, not liabilities. The more people can use what they know best, not just to adapt to the dominant culture, but to transform what is meant by dominant culture, the closer we can come to democracy's ideal of a rich, diverse, endlessly inclusive community. People are often discouraged from foregrounding their cultures and traditions on the assumption that this will lead to a divisive separatism but, as Boyte points out, democratic communities "cannot build a future if they don't bring their past with them" (2004, p. 105).

Practicing Democratic Leadership

Learning democracy can only happen in the doing of democracy. The first step in this process is for leaders to make a public commitment to working democratically as communicators, learners, and collaborators. This means acknowledging that anyone is as likely to make a valuable contribution to the community as anyone else, including the designated leader. One of the main learning projects of democracy therefore is how to create communication channels that are open enough to invite those contributions and allow them to have the fullest possible impact on thinking and action within the group.

One provocative discussion of what learning democracy looks like is the model of leadership that political theorist Benjamin Barber (2000) introduced originally in a tribute to James MacGregor Burns. According to Barber a democratic leader helps people to see the connections within a group that build community. Democratic leaders keep a stimulating conversation going that incorporates many voices, supports fruitful collaborations, and allows everyone in the group to get practice as both leader and follower. One of the most important ways democracy is learned is through the intentional creation of open and inclusive systems of communication.

Leaders learning democracy think relatively little about their own individual contributions and a great deal about the best ways for others to add value. Such leaders encourage others to share their experiences and ideas, to develop their community-building skills, to become effective advocates for causes that matter. These leaders are learning how to make the most of the community's many strengths for everyone's benefit. Their job, in other words, is to make the group look good and to do good. When democracy works, it makes the group more inventive and creative than it otherwise would be.

The thing that most consistently blocks democracy is a lack of faith in the ability of people to control their own affairs, what Myles Horton in an interview with Bill Moyers called the extraordinary knowledge of the so-called ordinary, common people. The impulse for advantaged elites to see so-called ordinary people as irresponsible, hopelessly distracted, ideologically hoodwinked, and even dumb is very strong. Overcoming this impulse requires what Myles Horton (1990) viewed as a democratic trust in people's good judgment. This, in turn, requires leaders who are not afraid to unleash their followers and co-workers' energies and who are willing to take a chance with shared, interdependent models of community leadership. My experience supports Horton's—that when people's ability to run their own organizations and communities is taken seriously, they are highly effective, even inspiring in demonstrating their individual and collective commitment.

More problematic still is the enduring attraction we all have to what Mary Parker Follett (1919/1998) called "power-over leadership." People in hierarchical leadership positions often like being in charge and all that it entails—being on top, telling people what to do, controlling the flow of information, and enjoying the prestige that accompanies such loftiness. Consequently, they tend to focus on consolidating their power as opposed to doing what is best for the community as a whole. Wresting control from such power-over leaders is hugely challenging, as it appears to be in their interest to keep a tight rein on everything. People throughout history have risked their lives in the effort to democratize power. Less dramatically, they lose jobs, freedom of movement, prestige, or economic security in this effort.

Hierarchies generally get in the way of democratic processes. They are admittedly not always a problem; indeed, emergency rooms, union organizing, freedom movements, and guerilla (as well as conventional) armies depend on them to accomplish their objectives. But because hierarchies tend to limit participation, concentrate power in a few people, and discourage opposing ideas, there must be a democratic presumption against their comprising the preferred pattern of organization. Those favoring hierarchy who also claim to support democracy must be prepared to show why a hierarchy is advantageous to every member of the community, as well as the community as a whole (Shapiro, 2001).

Finally, it would be remiss not to observe that the mass of community, movement, or organizational members themselves can sometimes present the biggest obstacle when trying to move toward more democratic practices. People raised in hierarchical cultures (including the so-called open democracies of the West) and unaccustomed to democratic processes in their organizations and communities assume that decision making is not part of their responsibilities, and that open, democratic leaders are weak and indecisive. Getting people to participate, to assume leadership roles after decades of being told that their experience is meaningless and that their opinions do not count for anything can only be overcome by stubbornly sticking to democratic practices.

Furthermore, experience has taught many of us not to trust leaders to share power for the good of all. We can imagine scenarios in which we are urged to take the lead on important projects, only to have the rug pulled out from under us just as we begin to feel comfortable with leading. Most readers will probably have experienced the way an avowal of democratic process is really an excuse for leaders to dump on people's shoulders the bulk of the work and responsibilities that leaders themselves should be exercising. Many of us will also have experienced the injuries of counterfeit democracy—of participating in a supposedly open, democratically determined process that is actually being manipulated by leaders to support their own purposes and agendas. The very real histories that give people little reason to trust their leaders who are trying to work democratically requires those same leaders to exercise an almost superhuman persistence in the face of resistance born of disappointment and disillusionment. This disillusionment is almost entirely the result of dishonest, inauthentic leaders who claim to want democracy, but in the end really cannot tolerate it or understand how to make it real.

Perils and Pitfalls of Leading Democratically

The tyranny of the majority is a danger to democracy identified by liberals and critical theorists alike. From J. S. Mill to Herbert Marcuse the tendency of the majority to reach a premature foreclosure of necessary dissent has been recognized as the major trap to democratic process. Another peril of learning democracy is believing that it must be extended to every trivial nook and crevice of organizational and community life. Leaders who have not really thought through the value of democracy for promoting learning and fostering human growth think that even when it comes to the number of reams of paper to be ordered, when to call a coffee break, or what kind of cookies to provide, a vote must be taken or the people must be extensively consulted. This is a grave mistake.

The often excruciating deliberations that accompany democracy must be reserved for those issues and decisions that will empower people in a meaningful way and that have the potential to alter the quality of group existence. Using democratic processes every time a decision must be made, no matter how unimportant, is a surefire way to exhaust both the process and the people who keep it going. Good judgment about which issues to bring to the group as a whole, periodically monitored by small subcommittees, is an essential part of learning and leading democracy. Also, as Albert's (2004, 2006) work on participatory economics (parecon) explains, different models of decision making are appropriate for different situations. As a general rule, those most affected by a decision should have a greater say in its outcome.

A related peril is the problem of permitting the interminable discussion. Leaders of all kinds do have a responsibility to put a limit on the amount of time set aside to exchange views on an issue and to reach a decision. Again, if too much time is allotted for discussion and closure is put off for too long, frustration, exhaustion, and eventually hostility set in. Although it is always difficult to know how long a conversation should go on, democracy will be defeated if the group begins to develop the feeling that decisions are constantly sidestepped and discussion never leads to anything worthwhile.

Also perilous is the tendency of democratic leaders to quell honest and reasonable opposition to decisions, particularly when those decisions are supported by the vast majority of community members. Opposition to and dissent from the prevailing views and practices of any community is basic to democracy. Dissent allows for alternative perspectives to be heard that may, in time, become the widely accepted practice. It also helps community members to see issues in a new light that, though it may not result in reversing decisions, nevertheless leads to subsequent decisions that are sounder and wiser.

Conclusion

Despite all the potential problems associated with learning and leading democracy, I argue that it provides the best setting for people to talk, think, and act together. In its commitment to hearing every voice, honoring every person's experience, making the most of everyone's strengths, and turning the strengths of the many into a powerful force for positive change, democracy knows no peer. Less a way of governing ourselves and more a way of learning to use our diversity to live and lead together, democracy, more than any other set of processes, helps us to answer questions about who we are and where we should go. It asserts that each of us is worthy of full inclusion and that no one lacks the capacity to guide others. It poignantly reminds us of how much is lost when some are cast aside and when others are denied what they need to become their best selves. It demands of us that we do more—for our neighbors, for our nearby communities, for distant unknown others—always in pursuit of a shared good and in quest of those things that promote social justice and human flourishing.

In a very real sense, democracy is self-interest writ large. It is the environment, the processes, the commitments, the goals that we would want for ourselves and our families extended to everyone—known and unknown, alike and unlike. Democracy is how Myles Horton lived his life. As he put it, "I do think if I have an idea, if I believe something, I've got to believe it's good for everybody. It can't be just good for me. [Similarly], you can't have an individual right. It has to be a universal right. I have no rights that everybody else doesn't have. There's no right I could claim that anybody else in the world can't claim, and I have to fight for their exercising that right just like I have to fight for my own" (Horton and Freire, 1990, pp. 105–106). Like Myles, I view democracy as a struggle not just for others but even more fundamentally a struggle for our own humanity.

References

Albert, M. *Parecon: Life After Capitalism*. London: Verso, 2004.

Albert, M. *Realizing Hope: Life Beyond Capitalism*. New York: ZED, 2006.

Baldwin, J. *Notes of a Native Son*. Boston: Beacon Press, 1955.

Barber, B. *A Passion for Democracy*. Princeton, NJ: Princeton University Press, 2000.

Boyte, H. C. *Everyday Politics: Reconnecting Citizens and Public Life*. Philadelphia: University of Pennsylvania Press, 2004.

Du Bois, W.E.B. *Dusk of Dawn, An Essay Toward An Autobiography of a Race Concept*. New York: Schocken Books, 1971.

Follett, M. P. *The New State: Group Organization as the Solution of Popular Government*. University Park, Penn.: Pennsylvania State University Press, 1919/1998.

Follett, M. P. *Creative Experience*. New York: Longmans, Green and Co., 1924.

Grace, A. P., and Rocco, T. S. (eds.). Challenging the Professionalization of Adult Education: John Ohliger and Contradictions in Modern Practice. San Francisco: Jossey-Bass, 2009.

Guy, T. C., and Brookfield, S. D. "W.E.B. Du Bois's Basic American Negro Creed and the Associates in Negro Folk Education: A Case Study of Repressive Tolerance in the Censorship of Radical Black Discourse on Adult Education." *Adult Education Quarterly*, 2009, *60*(1), 65–76.

Habermas, J. *Between Facts and Norms: Contributions to a Discourse Theory of Democracy*. Cambridge, Mass.: MIT Press, 1996.

Horton, M. *The Long Haul: An Autobiography*. New York: Teachers College Press, 1990.

Horton, M., and Freire, P. *We Make the Road by Walking: Conversations on Education and Social Change*. Philadelphia: Temple University Press, 1990.

Mezirow, J. *Transformative Dimensions of Adult Learning*. San Francisco: Jossey-Bass, 1990.

Shapiro, I. *Democratic Justice*. New Haven, Conn.: Yale University Press, 2001.

Sunstein, C. *The Second Bill of Rights: FDR's Unfinished Revolution and Why We Need It More Than Ever*. New York: Perseus Books, 2006.

STEPHEN BROOKFIELD *is Distinguished University Professor at the University of St. Thomas in Minneapolis-St. Paul.*

2

Drawing on examples from adult writing groups the authors have taught in marginalized communities in Chicago and Minneapolis, they present an egalitarian approach to teaching and learning that promotes democracy and eliminates hierarchical roles and relationships in classrooms and other educational settings.

Democracy Is in the Details: Small Writing Groups Prefiguring a New Society

Janise Hurtig, Hal Adams

Having written and read in a group, it leaves me with the sensation of having strengthened even more our bonds of friendship . . . I appreciate them, and I also thank them for having shared something about themselves with the group through their writings: the group that I feel happy to be a part of; the group with which I can get nervous, happy, sad; where I can cry, without fear, without embarrassment . . .

> —From "The Experience of Writing" by Dolores Nava (2002),
> parent writer at a small community school

When I first came to the writing group I was very shy. I didn't like to speak in public because I didn't think I had anything important to say. By writing in the group I have learned from my classmates that the experiences I have lived are interesting. They are also important. I can see that I have many stories to tell about my life that I think others can learn from. Now, I like to go to public forums to speak out about issues in our community, because I am confident in what I know and what I think...

> —From "My Experience in the Writing Group" by Flora Salinas,
> parent writer at a neighborhood school (unpublished)

In my opinion the greatest strength of the . . . Greek ancient democracy, was that it achieved a balance between the individual and the community that was never achieved before or since. That is one of the fundamental problems of politics: what is the relation of the individual, his rights, his liberties, his freedom, his possibilities of progress to the community in which he lives as a part.

> —James, 1973, p. 5

NEW DIRECTIONS FOR ADULT AND CONTINUING EDUCATION, no. 128, Winter 2010 © 2010 Wiley Periodicals, Inc.
Published online in Wiley Online Library (wileyonlinelibrary.com) • DOI: 10.1002/ace.387

15

The title of this chapter was inspired by a conversation that transpired during a community writing workshop Janise was teaching to parents of children who attended a neighborhood elementary school located in an immigrant Latino neighborhood in Chicago. We were discussing the stories participants had written the previous week in response to the theme "A leader who inspires me," prompted by the upcoming Martin Luther King Jr. holiday. Some participants had written about political figures or community organizers who had inspired them to participate in struggles for immigrant or worker rights; others had written about individuals who might not be considered leaders in the conventional sense, but who had the capacity to bring people together to work toward a common cause. Andrea wrote a piece in which she characterized her grandmother as a leader because of her ability to hold their large family together, keeping the peace among relatives who did not always see eye to eye. Marta chose as her model of a great leader the school's parent coordinator who was responsible for organizing the writing workshop and other parent programs at the school. Marta wrote, "I consider Doña Esperanza a great leader even though she does not really lead, at least not in the way we usually think about that word. She does not stand over us telling us what we should do. She does not exactly inspire us; she lets us inspire each other. She brings people together and lets all of us make common decisions. So everyone is equal."

The writing prompted the workshop participants to draw distinctions between the leadership practices of conventionally recognized leaders and others who were not necessarily recognized for their leadership. One participant declared that most conventional leaders are hypocrites. "There are so many so-called leaders that talk about equality, about democracy. But in their practice they are not democratic because they want to lead and us to follow. They want to have all the power and all the glory." Marta returned to her example of Doña Esperanza. "That is why she is a true leader. She doesn't just say we are all equal, she treats us that way. She encourages all of us to lead together. She is a true leader because her actions are consistent with her values." Responding to Marta's observations, Claudia offered the following: "So for me what Marta is saying is that all those words like leadership, or justice, or democracy, they sound like big ideas, things that depend on people with power. But really we are the ones who make those things happen. It depends on the way we act every day with each other, with our children, our husbands. What makes a real difference are the small things we do, the details."

The propositions these women put forth, emerging clearly from their experience, are really quite radical: namely, that the sources of social transformation can be found in the details of ordinary people's everyday practices, and that these practices should model the world we are working to create. These propositions, and the dialogic process through which the three women came to their understanding of leadership, convey the essence of what the Community Writing Project (CWP) seeks to enact as a form of

New Directions for Adult and Continuing Education • DOI: 10.1002/ace

popular education. Popular education, often referred to as "education for liberation," is based in the understanding that liberation is a praxis entailing people's ongoing critical reflection and action upon the world (Freire, 1971, p. 66). In other words, liberation is not an accomplishment or end result; rather, it is an ongoing, collective process. By extension, the work of creating a more democratic and egalitarian society occurs through collective practices that express and prefigure such a society (Gramsci, 1971). The work of popular education is one such practice.

It is a principle of popular education that the sources of imagination and insight into how to create a better society are to be found in the critical insights and creative expressions of the oppressed classes. As Bill Ayers (1995) put it, paraphrasing the work of Miles Horton, "the people with the problems are also the people with the solutions" (p. 35). In contrast to the deficit frameworks of mainstream education that portray the oppressed as objects of history, inadequate to the task of self-determination, popular education redeems the oppressed to their rightful position as subjects of history. Thus, popular educators recognize that the oppressed classes, through their experience of and struggle against oppression, have access to the insights and imagination that guide us toward a more just society (Freire, 1971; James, 1973). However, those insights are not always readily accessible. In *Pedagogy of the Oppressed* (1971), the Brazilian radical educator Paolo Freire characterized mainstream education as "banking education," a "top-down approach to knowledge transmission through which the teacher is sole dispenser of knowledge and the students are its passive recipients" (Mayo, 1999, p. 59). The antidemocratic, authoritarian pedagogies that characterize banking education are among the cultural practices the dominant classes use to repress the critical, creative exploration, and self-expression of oppressed people, in part by conveying to learners that they have no prior knowledge or expertise to contribute to their own education, let alone to the education of the group. Such a message, intrinsically dehumanizing and disenfranchising, conveys to ordinary people that they have no stories to tell, no wisdom to impart, no counsel to offer back to their communities.

It becomes the role of popular educators to create educational spaces in which members of oppressed groups come together to reflect on their lives, give voice to their individual and collective experiences within and beyond the classroom, and find value in the stories they tell about those experiences. Such spaces are fundamentally democratic and dialogic, in which "the learner assumes the role of knowing subject in dialogue with the educator" (Freire, 1985, p. 49). In this way, learning becomes a dialectical process of distancing oneself from one's experiences and the dominant perspectives about those experiences to examine them critically. Through such critical examination, people who have perceived themselves as objects of history recognize their agency in the world. They also gain an understanding of how the imposition of dominant worldviews contributes to their alienation from that recognition. The popular education classroom must also be a space in which learners feel respected and thus safe to take risks. As Freire put it, "it is a courageous endeavor to demythologize reality, a process through which men [sic] who had previously been submerged in reality begin to emerge in order to reinsert themselves into it with critical awareness." The small, personal narrative writing and publishing workshops we teach through the Community Writing Project aim to offer such a space (Adams and Hurtig, 2002).

For over 15 years, the CWP has formed partnerships with neighborhood schools and community groups to host writing workshops for adults living in marginalized conditions. Most workshops meet for about ten weeks, during which time participants write stories based in their experience, read and discuss them with the group, and edit a selection of their writings for publication in an issue of the magazine *Real Conditions*. The writing workshop sessions follow an apparently simple format, in which the writing that the workshop participants submit becomes the content of the workshop, and the group's discussion of the writing generates prompts for that session's writing. But every detail of the writing workshop pedagogy has a purpose: the ways the teacher comments on the participants' writing, the nature of group discussion of each person's story, the selection of writing prompts that respond to issues the group has explored, the process of collective editing for publication, and the distribution of a magazine of the writers' work. Each facet of the writing workshop method aims to foster collaborative learning relationships; celebrate self-expression; support critical and creative reflection on the world; recognize participants as intellectuals, artists, and leaders of their communities; and encourage the exploration of individual and collective action toward change. The excerpts from two parent writers that open this chapter convey their experience of this process. Through the sharing of stories, workshop members come to celebrate the unique contribution each participant makes to the group, while respecting the value of the workshop group as a community of writers. In this way the writing workshop seeks to strike the kind of balance between individual and community that are fundamental to democracy—as the opening quotation from C.L.R. James conveys.

Just as important, the pedagogy and methods of small writing workshops aim to engage teachers and learners in a process through which the students become educators themselves, actively adopting the workshop's democratic pedagogical practices and principles. We saw this sharing of the educative role in the opening story as the group explored the definition of leadership collectively and came to a mutual decision. The group, which had been meeting for several weeks at the time of that conversation, took charge of the content of their discussions and the decisions about the themes they would use as writing prompts each week. Popular educators have written extensively on educational practices through which a democratic classroom can be created such that teachers and students bring distinct knowledge and experience to the classroom and learn from each other.

New Directions for Adult and Continuing Education • DOI: 10.1002/ace

The focus tends to be on the roles and relationships of teacher and learners that foster dialogue, shared learning, and the coming into subjective self-awareness of the adult learner. Thus, while rightly insisting on the unique knowledge and insight that adult students bring to the classroom, descriptions of popular education classrooms tend to preserve the role distinctions of teacher and learner, rarely discussing the process by which the educative role is handed over to the students, such that learners become each others' teachers. This transformation, whereby students also become teachers, is an important element in establishing the classroom as an egalitarian space. Moreover, by affording participants the opportunity to take on the role of educator, they acquire the experience and confidence to become teachers of other workshops, bringing their expertise back into the community.

The purpose of this chapter is to explore the intersection of these three facets of the CWP's small writing workshops that are at the core of its democratic practice: legitimating the experiences and stories of ordinary people as expressions of their cultural work in the world; fostering a mutual relationship of the individual and the group; and the transitional process by which the role of educator is increasingly assumed by the group, such that learning and teaching occur as a free exchange of ideas. In these ways popular education leaps from being a humanistic, progressive approach to education to providing a vision, however modest, of an egalitarian world. In the rest of the chapter we tell two stories from writing workshops we have taught to adults in marginalized communities of Chicago and Minneapolis. Each of the stories describes moments in which the writing group participants help an individual member recognize the value and significance of their story while collectively supporting the writing workshop as a democratic learning community, often moving fluidly between their roles as students/learners and teachers/educators. We conclude the chapter by reflecting on some of the challenges that we have faced in our efforts to create democratic educational spaces within writing workshops.

Everyone Contributes and Everyone Responds

The following story from a parent writing workshop Hal taught at Wright High School shows how the members of a workshop created an egalitarian learning community by supporting a new writer's entrance into the group's writing and storytelling activities.

The writing workshop for parents had been meeting since school opened in early September. Debra, the mother of a tenth grader, attended her first class in late October. She listened and watched, but did not contribute any comments as the group members wrote and discussed their stories. The process must have been interesting to her because she remained attentive, but she was confused about the lack of direction given by the teacher. "What's the topic?" she asked more than once. Hal explained, as he did at the beginning of each writing period that at this phase of the writing members were doing "free-writing," that is, writing with the barest of an idea, and seeing what would happen. "See what you write yourself into," he said. "Don't pass judgment on your work at this point. Let it flow." "Like what?" Debra persisted. Hal responded, "Something small perhaps, like what you saw this morning on the way to class, an observation about a person you care about, an old family story, something you own that has meaning to you. It can be funny, sad, joyful, tragic—whatever you'd like."

Finally, in frustration, Debra turned to the group and asked, "How do I start?" By asking the workshop that important, earnest question, she took a step toward joining the group on the group's terms: namely, that a person must take initiative to join in. At this point, the rest of the class put down their pencils and gave their attention to Debra. Someone said to her, "Tell us a story." She stopped and started a few times as she talked her way into a story about her sister who died as a teenager. The story developed as Debra talked. "My sister was fourteen when she died. It hit us all hard. I guess death is always that way. We miss her so much." Some in the group jotted down notes; some asked questions. "How long ago was this?" "Where were you?" "Who was there?" Her classmates attended to her words with care and without judgment.

After a while, through the interchange with the group, Debra's story grew longer and more complex. She added characters, developed them, included dialogue, changed settings, and so on. "It's been five years. She would have gone to college by now. She was the smartest of us all. My mother cared for us all, but she favored our dead sister. Mother was the strongest of all at the end. She told us to remember, 'God has called her now and has left us to carry on.' But carrying on wasn't easy for some of us." Debra's initial question, "Where do I start," now became its opposite, "Where do I stop?" Sensing that the story was growing long and needed some focus, another student interrupted and asked Debra about her last statement. "Tell us more about carrying on. Who had the most trouble?" The whole group then took up Debra's story and worked with her on developing it. They asked questions, they made observations, they shared similar stories. Finally, the group complimented Debra and thanked her for a story they found compelling.

Not by being told, but by participating, Debra had learned a key principle of a democratic pedagogy, namely, that everybody contributes and everybody responds. By the time Debra told her first story to the group, the other students already understood that they, and not only the teacher, were responsible for the direction the class took and for transferring that information to each other. It was the group, not the teacher, that had taught Debra how to join in.

Debra's initiation demonstrates the advantage of a learning situation in which the students collectively take on a leadership role. On her first day participating in the workshop, Debra had a chance to observe through the group's consideration of her story that her experience was complex, profound, and unique. At the same time, it was universal, and prompted an engaging discussion about death, family, adversity, and healing. That discussion came from the workshop members as they combined their individual perceptions to show how the group's collective experience was relevant to Debra's story. In this way, participants in small writing groups are encouraged to realize that profound ideas about the world can come from their individual experience and the pooled experience of people like themselves. It need not come from people they consider to be experts. Indeed, it shows them that they are the experts when it comes to their own lives. The workshop members' response to Debra showed her that she had introduced a topic the whole group could grasp and discuss in depth. The workshop members explored the universal elements of an individual's real story, and made sense of life events that can be overwhelming when considered only in isolation from other people.

This interactive approach to telling and writing stories is sometimes referred to as "giving counsel" (see Benjamin, 1969). It can happen only when people engage in oral or written verbal exchanges. Giving counsel and storytelling never happens in isolation. The process, by definition, is communal, democratic, and egalitarian. This is education as we define it in our writing groups.

A Community of Equals

In the basement of a parish rectory that now houses Project Change, a community education and outreach center that serves a predominantly Latino immigrant neighborhood in Chicago, a group of eight Latina women are meeting with Janise to write and share stories about their lives. They also are talking about the writing group's process. It is their fourth meeting.

The session begins like most workshop sessions. Janise returns to the writers the pieces they had written at the previous session, replete with her written comments. The comments include affirmations of what was written, questions prompted by the writing, suggestions to expand the writing, and identification of compelling aspects of the story. The comments have several functions: they demonstrate that the teacher has learned from the writers' stories, model a pedagogy based in constructive and supportive feedback, and encourage the writers to develop their writing. At the same time, Janise provides a computer printout of all the stories so the participants can read along as each writer reads her work aloud.

After the writers have spent a few minutes reviewing their writing, Janise invites the first writer to read her story to the rest of the class. Maria volunteers. Janise asks the class to listen attentively to Maria's story. She reminds the group members that, after the author reads the story, they will have the responsibility of offering feedback on the story's content. Usually when it comes time to write, the teacher suggests two or three writing prompts based on issues the group has discussed. She also solicits writing prompt ideas from the group. In this way, the content of the class emerges from the group's creative work of writing and discussion. However, at the previous session Janise had deviated from this practice. She proposed that the participants write about a place that had positive associations. She suggested they include detailed descriptions and significant characters within the story. She offered this prompt to encourage participants to write with great detail, as a way of supporting the development of their writing craft, and as a way of emphasizing that the insights and opinions we develop are based in the details of our experiences.

Maria reads a story about how every morning she and her father would go up to the roof of the house to feed the pigeons and rabbits that they kept in cages made of cloth and wire. She describes how her father fashioned the cages so that he could feed the birds and rabbits water and a bit of grain. Alicia points out that by describing the two of them doing something meaningful together, namely feeding the pigeons, Maria managed, without ever saying so, to convey how meaningful that time with her father was. Some participants point out words or passages they found especially striking. Others respond to Maria's account with similar stories from their childhood experiences of keeping animals as food or pets.

When Janise asks who would like to read next, the other writers are hesitant. Finally Martha says, "No one else wants to read. I can read mine. But I'm not sure I completed the assignment correctly. My story doesn't have a lot of details the way Maria's does." The group responds supportively to Martha's expression of insecurity, offering an alternative perspective on the writing assignment and the value of her work. "There's no such thing as a correct way in the writing workshop," they comment. "We want to hear your story the way you choose to write it." Martha acknowledges the encouragement and is emboldened to read her story about her family's ritual weekend gatherings in the patio of her aunt's home, which she describes with vivid detail.

As soon as Martha finishes the other writers begin to comment on her story. Rosario offers a comment that seems to respond to Martha's fear that her story was not detailed enough. "Your descriptions make us feel like we are on that patio." There is a flurry of discussion about the familial sensibility Martha has conveyed through her writing, and about numerous stories from other writers about family spaces or reunions. As the discussion subsides, Sandra returns to Martha's earlier comment about having gotten the assignment wrong. "The writing themes are meant to get people writing. Whatever you write is important, because it is your experience. Besides, it is interesting to see how different people respond to a writing theme."

This interchange among the writers exemplifies the kind of democratic work the workshop community engages in by recognizing the unique experiences and expressions of each individual and the value those expressions have for the rest of the group. In doing so, this group of writers took responsibility for creating a space in which participants were able to develop new ways of engaging in the learning process. Martha had responded to the praise Maria's story received based on old classroom learning habits; that is, by comparing herself to another classmate. When Martha compared her story to Maria's, she found her story lacking. The writing workshop is based on noncompetitive, nonhierarchical relationships among learners and teachers, such that the classroom is recast as a community of equals in which each person is unique in what they bring to the learning environment. When Martha reacted based on old habits of competition, the writing group collectively reassured her that her writing was equally valuable and important. In doing so, they had also taken on the role of teacher.

Is a Democratic Classroom Enough? Small Group Writing as the Basis for Community Action

There is a passage in Paolo Freire's (1985) *The Politics of Education* in which he identifies the liberatory role of literacy when it is a creative and critical act. He also identifies the limits of critical literacy, noting that "without any illusion of triggering liberation, it will nevertheless contribute to its process" (p. 17). Freire's comments could be interpreted as meaning that the educative work that takes place in democratic classrooms like the small writing workshops initiates a stage in the process of liberation, but is not the end in itself. This formulation could be read as either contradicting or refining another proposition of Freire's we presented at the beginning of this chapter, namely that liberation occurs through the process of working toward it.

For Freire and other radical educators, the kind of critical reflection on experience that takes place in the writing workshops is one phase of the cyclical process of exploration of an issue, critical discussion and reflection on the issue, and the taking of action based on that discussion . . . followed by another cycle of exploration of the issue and the actions taken. Nina Wallerstein and Elsa Auerbach (2004) refer to this cycle as "participatory praxis" (p. 13). This model of education for liberation poses a conundrum when we think about the role of small writing workshops in the larger movement for human liberation that certainly requires participatory praxis. On the one hand, we have never framed the writing workshops as action-oriented. That is, we consider the activity of writing and publishing to be the goal of the workshops. On the other hand, there are instances in which group members, either collectively or individually, are moved to take action on an issue that comes up in the group.

One such action was taken by members of a group Hal taught to parents in the elementary school their children attended, located adjacent to a massive public housing complex where many of the writers lived. During the city's relentless dismantling of the projects, the group members' stories often concerned their fears about the uncertainty of their housing situation. For several years, Tandra, one of the writers, and her family had lived rent-free because her husband James had a verbal agreement with the Chicago Housing Authority (CHA) to be on call 24/7 to do emergency maintenance in their building. When the informal maintenance agreement was rescinded, CHA officials extended permission to the family to remain in the building.

Then, Tandra and James received an eviction notice. They were the last family remaining in a condemned, thirteen-story building. The isolation in itself was frightening, but the prospect of being homeless was worse. CHA officials now claimed they were squatters. An earlier court order required CHA to give a year's notice of eviction to those who held leases on their apartments. Because of the informal but verbally sanctioned agreements, Tandra and her family had no lease. The eviction notice gave them three weeks to evacuate, or CHA would remove the family and their belongings. They had the right to appeal within a week. It seemed they were doomed, but Tandra's writing group, along with the school principal, had not yet swung into action.

On the morning of the hearing, group members, the school principal, Tandra, and James took the "El" to housing court in downtown Chicago. When their case was called, the principal, Hal, and one group member accompanied Tandra and James to the bench. Tandra and James presented their case persuasively. The judge noted the presence in court of community members, and the Johnson's long-standing record of service to the school and community. She rejected the CHA lawyer's argument. "These people aren't squatters," she said. "They're a central part of this school and residential community." She ordered the CHA to give them their rightful year's notice of eviction. She urged Tandra and James to strike a bargain with CHA, which was eager to clear out the last family from a building that was scheduled for immediate demolition. CHA gave them a moving allowance and an apartment in another building not scheduled for demolition for some time. It was no ultimate solution to poverty and housing issues, but it provided some much needed breathing room.

To offer another example, parents have periodically compared the writing workshop practice in which the instructors offer enthusiastic comments on participants' writing in purple, green, or blue ink, with classroom teachers' uses of "red ink" to correct and markup writing. Through the experience of receiving encouraging and engaging feedback on their writing, one group of parent writers were prompted to explore in stories and discussion, the ways their own teachers' use of red ink had intimidated them and alienated them from the writing process. Drawing on their childhood school experiences and critical discussion of the issue in the group, the parents came to perceive the approach those teachers were taking to their children's work as undermining their children's confidence in their writing, and discouraging

New Directions for Adult and Continuing Education • DOI: 10.1002/ace

them from doing their schoolwork. The writing and discussion led two parents to approach their children's teachers about the deleterious impact of "red ink" on their children's relationship to writing and to school work more generally. One writer presented the essay she had written, entitled "Red Ink," to her son's teacher.

Although we discuss and support the actions that writers choose to take as a result of participating in the group, we have never thought of the workshop process as a vehicle for organizing or advocacy work. We leave the reader with a series of questions we have posed to ourselves. Is it enough that the writing workshop serves as a model of a democratic society, a space in which past experiences and new possibilities can be freely explored? Is the lack of an explicitly action-oriented purpose to the group a shortcoming of the workshop method as a form of liberatory education? Or is it possible that the creative and critical activity of writing and publishing stories from the community is an instance of liberatory action in its own right?

References

Adams, H., and Hurtig, J. "Creative Acts, Critical Insights: Adult Writing Workshops in Two Chicago Neighborhoods." In E. Auerbach (ed.), *Community Partnerships, Case Studies in TESOL Practice Series*. Alexandria, Va.: TESOL, 2002.

Ayers, W. "A Dream That Keeps on Growing: Myles Horton and Highlander." *Democracy & Education*, 1995, 10(2), 34–36.

Benjamin, W. "The Storyteller." In H. Arendt (ed.), *Illuminations: Essays and Reflections*. New York: Harcourt Brace Jovanovich, 1969.

Freire, P. *Pedagogy of the Oppressed*. New York: Herder and Herder, 1971.

Freire, P. *The Politics of Education: Culture, Power, and Liberation*. South Hadley, Mass.: Bergin & Garvey, 1985.

Gramsci, A. *Selections from the Prison Notebooks*. New York: International Publishers, 1971.

James, C.L.R. *Modern Politics*. Detroit: Bewick Editions, 1973.

Mayo, P. *Gramsci, Freire, and Adult Education: Possibilities for Transformative Action*. London: Zed Books, 1999.

Nava, D. "The Experience of Writing." *Real Conditions*, 2002, 3(3), p. 22.

Wallerstein, N., and Auerbach, E. *Problem-Posing at Work: Popular Educator's Guide*. Edmonton, Canada: Grass Roots Press, 2004.

JANISE HURTIG is a senior researcher and co-director of the PRAIRIE Group, College of Education, at the University of Illinois at Chicago, where she is coordinator of the Chicago branch of the Community Writing and Research Project.

HAL ADAMS is coordinator of the Minneapolis branch of the Community Writing and Research Project. He retired from the College of Education at the University of Illinois at Chicago.

3

In an attempt to preserve the field's collective historical memory, the authors in this chapter explore participatory practices at the Open Book, an adult literacy program in Brooklyn, from 1985–2002. Students' roles in shaping those practices are examined and reflections on the possibilities for building democratic communities in literacy programs, particularly in the current context, are included.

"Everybody Had a Piece . . .": Collaborative Practice and Shared Decision Making at the Open Book

John Gordon, Dianne Ramdeholl

Although we are adults, we come to these programs because something in our lives didn't go right. Something didn't happen in school for us and we need encouragement. We need to hear you can do this, we need to hear it doesn't matter what level you are, you can bring yourself higher . . . we need someone to say you're not just another number passing through here, you're a complex human being and you came here with so many struggles and dreams. (Tonya, a student at the Open Book)

Slim and Thompson (1995) say that research which doesn't honor local knowledge is unlikely to succeed. Yet in New York City and elsewhere in the United States, federal and state adult literacy policies have focused increasingly on reductionist outcomes that deny local knowledge and experience. The National Reporting System for adult education defines student success primarily by standardized test scores and job placement. (Sparks and Peterson, 2000). Increasingly, conversations among practitioners about teaching have been reduced to how best to meet these demands. In this landscape there is no space to honor the complex realities Tonya invokes. Nowhere is there room to grapple with questions such as: As practitioners, how can we utilize students' voices to inform and shape our practice? How do we structure a learning environment to address students' lived realities?

Vincent, one of the primary architects of adult literacy policy in New York City, reflects on changes in policy within the last two decades.

NEW DIRECTIONS FOR ADULT AND CONTINUING EDUCATION, no. 128, Winter 2010 © 2010 Wiley Periodicals, Inc.
Published online in Wiley Online Library (wileyonlinelibrary.com) • DOI: 10.1002/ace.388

It felt like there was more space for progressive dialogue in the 80s. When we developed literacy funding proposals, they were rooted in progressive philosophies. In the 1980s the struggles were about building capacity that was high quality. We looked at all the key elements, not just federal accountability measures. We asked, "Do we have the voices of learners? Are we collaborating in ways that make the best use of resources? Can we strategically expand the resources available in equitable ways?" We were constantly asking people, "What do you think?" That's much less the case now. Before, funders and practitioners would talk about how we could make learning relevant to students' lives. How can that learning be transformational? How does it impact the community in ways that create more equity? Now that has changed. Data collection has come more to be seen as an accountability measure as opposed to informing policy and developing quality practices. The students' voice at the table and active participation has been totally lost or marginalized. Welfare reform also shifted things enormously. Literacy programs were forced to shift their focus from education to employment. Popular education, as practiced by the Open Book, without sufficient funding, will be marginalized forever . . .

Beginnings

On a cold January morning I walked into the basement of a local Catholic school in Brooklyn and taught the first class of the Open Book, a community literacy program created a month earlier by a local social service agency with a tiny sliver of funding from the city. I had only started work a week before and was the Open Book's first director and teacher (Gordon, 1991).

It was 1985. New York City was finally emerging from the economic crisis it suffered in the early 1970s, and Mayor Ed Koch had dedicated $35 million to fund literacy programs over a four-year period. The Open Book was one of them.

Although the initiative was broadly understood as part of a workforce development strategy, the funding was often justified in more humanistic terms, emphasizing everyone's right to literacy. By the early 1990s the tenor had changed; rather than a *right*, everyone had a *responsibility* to learn how to read so they could contribute to the economy. During the Clinton years, this would take on an even harder edge, as "welfare reform" essentially eliminated the right of public assistance recipients to participate in literacy programs. In 1998, with the passage of the Workforce Investment Act, literacy funding was explicitly tied to employment.

All that was in the future though, and in 1985 it was still possible to envision a literacy program that aimed to help people develop the tools to transform their lives and to engage with others to bring about social change.

There were about eight or nine students that first day. The basement was dark and dingy with a concrete floor. We didn't even have a room, just a space in the corner populated by a dozen child-sized desks and separated from the rest of the basement by a row of lockers. Every 15 minutes or so, a class of about twenty-five or thirty eight-year-olds would be led down into the basement by their teacher to go to the bathroom—en masse. Just about every kid would peek in between the lockers to see what was going on. The students were nervous and uptight, a little embarrassed because they didn't know how to read well. Most were sitting in a class for the first time in years. It certainly didn't help to have a group of giggling eight-year-olds looking in every fifteen minutes. But we carried on.

Pretty soon we got over our nervousness and found that we liked each other. Students began to tell each other their stories, to share what was going on in their lives, to talk about their pain and struggle, along with their hopes and dreams. Even though I didn't have any formal teacher experience, I had the sense to step back and give people the time and space to tell their stories, to talk to one another. Within a couple of months both the students and I began to feel that something special was happening. By that summer, the agency had found us our own space, a loft up the block. Students came in, and we painted and decorated the space together. A sense of community was building—kindled by the storytelling, the painting, the freedom students felt to talk about what was going on in their lives. (Gordon, 1991)

It was the students who consistently articulated the idea of the school as community and its centrality in the Open Book's mission. And it was the students, through their actions, who made that community real. As Maria, one of those early students said:

> What community means to me—to be there for others and to try to lift each other when we're down. Life is a community of caring and love and hope. My class is like that. It's a place where you can have friendship; you can feel warm and express who you are without being afraid to be you. There's an energy among each other, whatever we talk about. It could be family, kids, jobs, homeless, also teachers, doctors, and sickness. It's like an Open Book (Rosado, 1990).

From the beginning, teachers took time in classes each week to ask how things were going, what ideas students had for changes in the way we were working. Curriculum was always up for discussion. It was the teachers' job to put together coherent lessons, to create a plan for learning and development. But that plan, and particularly the instructional content, was understood to be a product of ongoing dialogue—sometimes formal, sometimes not—with the class.

Often, students would weigh in on class structure, perhaps wanting to start the day differently or to do math more often. Students would raise issues around lateness or attendance and would often propose stricter rules. These tended to be the most contentious discussions. We tried to talk them out as best we could, aiming for some kind of informal consensus.

> I went to other programs but I didn't even stay to register. I don't know why but I didn't feel like I belonged there. I would even make the registration

appointments but once I showed up I knew I couldn't go through with it. I would just run down the stairs and leave. I knew they were places I couldn't stay. But from the moment I went upstairs to the Open Book I saw people sitting at tables working in groups. It felt so free. I remember one group talking about everything they were going to do. I observed them talking and was so moved. After joining the program I became one of them. You couldn't shut me up! (Edna, a student)

By the second year, we had grown to four classes and began to have regular meetings of the school community. Each month, we would bring the two morning classes together for a school meeting. The director would usually bring items for the agenda, but anyone could, and did, add to it. Over time, these meetings covered a wide range of issues, from the mundane to the far-reaching: keeping the space clean, proposals for changes in our schedule and class offerings, ideas for new initiatives or applications for funding, a plan for students to evaluate teachers. A similar process went on in the evenings.

By and large, students responded well to the meetings, though some didn't want to participate. But however positive the response to the meetings, they were still run by the director and were usually, though not always, held on his initiative. As time went on, and the notion of shared decision making and student leadership solidified at the Open Book, more people took responsibility for the meetings, and they were sometimes led by students.

We were not the only program exploring student involvement in decision-making and student leadership. In 1988, a group of students and teachers from the Open Book attended a Student-Teacher Literacy conference at Lehman College and participated in a workshop given by students who were working as student-teachers at Bronx Educational Services. Afterwards, everyone was excited. On the ride home, the talk was, "Why don't we do that? We can do that!"

We felt that students working as assistant teachers could profoundly alter the way students and teachers understood the power dynamics in the classroom. Having students step into the role of teacher would undermine the notion that the important knowledge was stored in the brains of the teachers and affirm the knowledge and expertise of students, i.e., the community (Freire, 1970). As it happened, we had the perfect candidate—a student in our beginning class who was ready to move into the more advanced class. She was highly respected by the rest of the students and was already spending a lot of her time helping others. We talked it over in the class and among the staff and made the decision to hire her.

It was around that time that the notion of student leadership crystallized for us. Until then the collaborative, shared decision making we practiced had arisen organically out of the sense of community that had developed and out of students' desire to participate fully. We now had a core group of staff members and students who deeply identified with the school and believed in student leadership. The students moved things forward in two important ways: (1) they pushed the staff to involve students in every way, and (2) they began to take independent initiatives. They would stay after class and meet and talk, mostly informally. They organized a women's group that met after class once a week on their own. Basemah, a Palestinian student, began to invite Arabic women to meet with her at the school after class. A domestic violence survivor, Basemah started running support groups for Arabic women, many of whom were struggling with the same issues.

In 1988, in an effort to bridge the divide between the morning and evening classes, we formed the Student Teacher Council. We continued to hold school meetings during class time, but some people saw those as limited. The Student Teacher Council in theory had representatives from each class and met once a month on Saturdays. It met with mixed success. Attendance was always a struggle. The group did some important work, creating policies on smoking, developing guidelines for dealing with conflicts between students, deciding on some important new initiatives, and more. It provided a forum where some students developed leadership skills and communicated the message that we were serious about student involvement. Ultimately, though, it proved too difficult to sustain. After two years, we returned to our reliance on in-school meetings.

Perhaps our most far-reaching initiative was in hiring. Early on, we began to involve students in the process of hiring new staff, including teachers. Whenever we hired a new teacher, we would form a hiring committee made up of students and staff. Usually the committee would include about seven or eight students, mostly from the affected class, along with the director and a teacher. The group would conduct all the interviews together and then meet to make a decision.

> Staff and students would come together as one entity to make a decision on who we think would fit in our community. I never was involved in a process like that before in my entire life in all the schools. I've never even heard this being done before. The person would come in and we sat them down. Each student got a chance to ask the candidate questions, different scenarios. Once the person left, we would go back and talk about it. (Eugene, a student)

Most of these practices continued, along with others, until 2001 when the Open Book went under—a victim of the funding environment and the national shift toward the Workforce Investment Act goals.

Reflections

The model of student participation and collaborative decision making developed at the Open Book grew organically out of the sense of community created in the early years of the school. That sense of community was articulated consistently by students. They talked of the school as a family, a second home, a community—and in their practice they made that community a reality. Shared decision-making and democratic practices were an obvious and logical outgrowth of the community being built. We tried to open every important decision to the student body, including whom we hired, what the content of our program should be, what the class schedule looked like, and more.

Student writing and publishing was central to our curriculum. Each year we published one or two long student journals. In addition, we published four books of longer works, including oral histories. We believed that students had important things to say, to each other, to us, and to their community (Martin, 2000). Their writing was a contribution to a complex dialogue, inside and outside the Open Book, which documented the lives students led and explored key issues they faced. The oral histories and Edna's writings in particular recounted Open Book women's struggles with abuse and violence in their lives. They were read and discussed by succeeding generations of students and often passed on by students to family members and friends. In their stories, the women articulated a yearning for freedom that became touchstones for the Open Book community. This practice brought student voices and their life struggles into the center of the curriculum and was inseparable from our commitment to student involvement in decision making, to a democratic community (Auerbach, 1992).

The Open Book remains, for many of the students and staff involved, a defining experience in their lives, a time that allowed them to see different possibilities, for themselves and society. Edna articulates it this way:

> The Open Book changed my whole life. I felt like I opened a door and found everything I was looking for on the other side. It made me feel like a person, like I was somebody that I could do whatever I want. Now, people see me as someone who's smart and open. Before the Open Book I used to go to psychiatrists. I never told them an inch of my stories. Nothing! I didn't even know who I was. I knew my name was Edna but who was Edna? What did she want from life? . . . I used to be so closed before, so afraid, but somehow in the Open Book, I just let it all out. It was a place I could go and learn to trust, to let myself be me. We protected each others' words and values. I felt free to say and do what I wanted. There was a sense of safety and trust in the program and I knew that nobody could hurt me again. I knew that we would protect each other's words and I've taken those feelings with me.

Still, apart from the arguably enduring magic of the program, testified to by so many participants (Ramdeholl, 2010), what larger significance did the Open Book have for the lives of its students? To what extent was it a force for community change? What contribution did it make to movements for societal change?

New Directions for Adult and Continuing Education • DOI: 10.1002/ace

In another time and place, the Open Book might have been a resource for a popular struggle, a place where learning was tied to what people needed to know in order to prevail, a place where people could build skills for that struggle, a place that produced and nourished activists and helped them deepen their understandings of what they were doing.

Clearly, adult education, broadly defined, has played that role before. Brown (1990) has documented Septima Clark's experience organizing the Citizenship Schools in the South during the civil rights movement. In those schools, people came together to learn how to read and write to develop tools to overturn oppressive systems of power.

For the most part, that did not occur at the Open Book. Significant numbers of Open Book students did participate in citywide adult education rallies and meetings calling for more literacy funding or protesting "welfare reform" in the mid-1990s, but those efforts were largely led by teachers.

A significant exception involves the role of women at the school. Most of the students who played key leadership roles were women. Over the years, many women in abusive relationships came to the Open Book. Many of them wrote and talked about their experiences with domestic violence and the importance of the school as a source of support for them. In time, the school gained a reputation as a safe space and a resource for women struggling for autonomy and freedom in their lives (Ramdeholl, Evans, and Gordon, 2008).

> I see part of myself inside each woman the first time I meet them. I hope I can take some of their fear away. I share some of my experiences so they know they are not the only ones being abused. I dream someday of having a big house so women who are abused can get away. I dream of us working together and helping each other. I want all women to be able to stand up for themselves the way I did. (Roa, Jaber, and Ramirez, 1994)

We don't expect adult literacy programs to be starting points for social change. There may be times when a particular program will play that role, but mostly the catalysts for social movements will be outside literacy programs—no matter how good they are. Our capacity to contribute to those movements depends a lot on what is happening in the communities around us. During the civil rights movement, the citizenship schools (in many ways, literacy programs) played a key role in bringing people into action by helping them acquire the tools to organize. In 2010, in the absence of such a broad popular movement, the potential for literacy programs to contribute to those social movements is undeniably more limited.

Looking Ahead

> For me being a student at the Open Book was very empowering. It wasn't just a place where you sit in a classroom but a place where you can be a leader. . . .

> It wasn't just a staff school, it was for students and staff. We all had a hand in
> creating the Open Book. Everybody had a piece of the Open Book pie. That's
> something schools don't do…. (Eugene)

In its practice and stance, the Open Book represented an implicit critique of the dominant culture. As a space where participants could establish egalitarian and participatory relationships, values, and ways of being and relating, the Open Book embodied an alternative to the hierarchy and enforced passivity of daily life. In the process of learning to read and write, students and staff fashioned their own forms of decision making and community building. Those forms were nonhierarchical and built around informal consensus. In a society structured around top-down decision making, where individual civic activity, especially by poor people, is generally limited to voting, and participation in social service programs is framed within a professional–client relationship, Open Book students took on active and leading roles in shaping the program.

What role do such places play in undermining the status quo, in creating a sense of hope and possibility? Graeber (2007) has argued that it is precisely in such sites, "in the spaces in-between," that democratic alternatives get built. Is it delusional (or, worse, self-aggrandizing) to imagine that an adult education program funded by federal workforce development dollars and run by a social service agency might play a role in building alternatives to a system based on hierarchy and privilege? Perhaps. But we would argue that wherever we are, we need to find the cracks in which to work and the possibilities for inviting students into authentic and sincere democratic activity. For adult education to consistently foster democracy, space must be made to include students' voices at every level of program planning, decision making and policy, and participatory practices should be explicitly connected to instruction (Shor, 1980).

We also believe it is essential to situate adult literacy within the long history of freedom struggles connected to class, race, and gender. Now is no time to nurture historical amnesia. If adult literacy in large part is about redefining what's possible in people's lives, then students' concerns and perspectives should be at the center of programs. In that vein, adult education practices must legitimize learners' lives, perspectives, discourses, and voices. Writing and publishing oral histories is one way to make space for people to tell their stories in their own words and to open those stories up to the community.

Student stories, seen in this light, can bring a fresh, bottom-up perspective to questions of politics, culture, and history. They provide vehicles for students to critically examine commonly accepted concepts of truth and depictions of reality. They offer an opportunity to scrutinize unseen voices and underlying agendas that are rarely visible in texts. Unpacking these concepts can lead to deconstructing beliefs about power (who benefits from the maintenance of the status quo?) as well as students' own ideas about their schooling and feelings of self-blame imposed by the dominant culture.

Finally, we argue that engaging in participatory models in a sincere and committed way demands that we scrutinize our own underlying assumptions so that we do not inadvertently replicate and perpetuate current power relationships rooted in paternalistic colonization, and instead labor together towards a more egalitarian, humane world.

References

Auerbach, E. *Making Meaning Making Change*. Washington, DC: Center for Applied Linguistics, 1992.

Brown, C. S. *Ready from Within: Septima Clark and the Civil Rights Movement*. Trenton, N.J.: Africa World Press, 1990.

Freire, P. *Pedagogy of the Oppressed*. New York: Seabury Press, 1970.

Gordon, J. "We're All in This Together: Leadership and Community at the Open Book by Staff and Students at the Open Book." Unpublished manuscript, the Open Book, Brooklyn, 1991.

Graeber, D. *Possibilities: Essays on Hierarchy, Rebellion, and Desire*. Oakland, Calif.: AK Press, 2007.

Martin, R. *Listening Up*. Portsmouth, N.H.: Heinemann, 2000.

Ramdeholl, D. *Adult Literacy in a New Era: Oral Histories from the Open Book*. Boulder. Colo.: Paradigm Publishers, 2010.

Ramdeholl, D., Evans, S., and Gordon, J. "Making a Beach: Women, Community, and Democracy at the Open Book." In M. Miller and K. King (eds.), *Empowering Women through Literacy* (pp. 221–232). Charlotte, N.C.: Information Age Publishing, 2008.

Roa, E., Jaber, B., and Ramirez, I. "I see a Part of Myself." Unpublished manuscript, the Open Book, Brooklyn, 1994.

Rosado, M. "Where the Sun Shines Every Day." In *Stories from the Heart: Writings from the Open Book* (p. 1). Unpublished manuscript, the Open Book, Brooklyn, 1990.

Shor, I. *Critical Teaching and Everyday Life*. Chicago: University of Chicago Press. 1980.

Slim, H., and Thompson, P. *Listening for a Change*. Philadelphia: New Society Publishers, 1995.

Sparks, B., and Peterson, E. "Adult Basic Education and the Crisis of Accountability." In A. Wilson and E. Hayes (eds.), *Handbook of Adult and Continuing Education* (pp. 263–275). San Francisco: Jossey-Bass, 2000.

John Gordon was the director of education at the Open Book from 1985–2001. He is currently associate vice president of programs at the Fortune Society in New York City.

Dianne Ramdeholl is currently an assistant professor in education at the Harry Van Arsdale Jr. Center for Labor Studies and Graduate Studies at Empire State College in New York City. She was an instructor at the Open Book.

New Directions for Adult and Continuing Education • DOI: 10.1002/ace

The author describes how the political struggles of immigrant domestic workers challenge the destructive logic of a global capitalist patriarchy. It offers a theory of radically democratic learning centered on a collective sense of being-in-relation, and therefore of assuming responsibility for protecting life and its conditions.

4

Radically Democratic Learning in the Grounded In-Between

Mechthild Hart

What have we done to democracy? What have we turned it into? What happens once democracy has been used up? When it has been hollowed out and emptied of meaning? What happens when each of its institutions has metastasized into something dangerous? What happens now that democracy and the Free Market have fused into a single predatory organism with a thin, constricted imagination that revolves almost entirely around the idea of maximizing profit? Is it possible to reverse this process? Can something that has mutated go back to being what it used to be?

Is there life after democracy? (Roy, 2009)

Arundhati Roy asks profoundly unsettling questions about liberal representative democracy, our Western working model. She bases her critique on its failures, its having gone wrong where it once was right. In other words, she sees the fusion of the free market economy with the political system and its turning into a global predatory organism as the symptom of a disease caught by a once healthy body. However, if she had drawn the "deep structure" (von Werlhof, 2001) of capitalism and democracy into her critique she would not simply have asked whether it was possible for democracy to "go back to what it used to be." Instead, she would have seen that liberal democracy and capitalism have always been bedfellows, with neoliberalism and neocolonialism their most recent offspring. In other words, as a *capitalist* democracy it has not just gone wrong but has been pursuing rather unerringly the same fundamental logic. The erosion of civil society

NEW DIRECTIONS FOR ADULT AND CONTINUING EDUCATION, no. 128, Winter 2010 © 2010 Wiley Periodicals, Inc.
Published online in Wiley Online Library (wileyonlinelibrary.com) • DOI: 10.1002/ace.389

and its various democratic institutions has been following this logic, as has the relentless destruction of the conditions of life, resulting in social–cultural and ecological disasters of increasingly global proportions. Liberal democracies still contain political advantages and civic freedoms, at least those which are still standing, but the Western logic of progress and development no longer functions as its economic undercurrent. Instead, it has risen to the surface and has become a raging and ever-widening river, uprooting, drowning everything living in its path.

In this chapter I therefore start my examination of democratic learning by responding to Roy's question, "Is there life after democracy?" with, "Most likely not if we do not probe into what has been making it move in tandem with more and more destructive socioeconomic forces." I therefore ask instead, "What kinds of democratic relations to each other and to non-human nature would counter such life-destroying logic? And what radically democratic forms of learning would not only dismantle the destructive logic, but also engage the learners in slowly building a different one, one that embraces our dependence on the earth, our embodiedness, our being in relation with all living and non-living things on earth?" I will use my involvement in the political struggles of immigrant domestic workers as the foundation of both a critique of the destructive logic of global capitalist relations as well as a description of actual and possible learning processes that challenge this logic, and that begin replacing it with a different, life-affirming one.

The Life-Destroying Logic of a Global Capitalist Patriarchy

Despite many life-changing global political and economic upheavals during the past three decades, one element has nevertheless always stayed the same: Domestic work is women's work, regardless of its many different names, and regardless of the broad spectrum of activities and working conditions to which it may refer. Maids, household laborers, cleaning ladies, housekeepers, babysitters, companions for the elderly, or nannies all do "women's work," and culturally and nationally different variations of hierarchical man-woman relations smoothly feed into each other to keep it that way. As so tellingly illustrated by the term "working mother," what women do in the house is not real work but something else. In one way or other, this something else always comes in contact with the "blood, guts and gore" that leak out of messy bodies (Klein, 1999, p.196). People need to eat, digest, and sleep, their various bodily functions need to be catered to, and the messes they inevitably make have to be cleaned up. This makes the work undeserving of public acknowledgment, and translated into economic terms, it makes it undeserving of a living wage (see Hart, 2005).

The deep structure of Western free market economies and liberal democracies is wedded to patriarchal value systems that arise out of a particular way of thinking about and relating to the physical and material foundations of life.

This thinking is wedded to a Cartesian dualistic framework that makes it "suffer from the desire to be disembodied" (Bauman, 2003, p. 52). María Lugones (2003) calls this desire the "love for purity," where "pure" equals white and disembodied. The color white is unsullied by the earth, one's body, and body-to-body contact with the nonwhite, the impure, those closer to nature. The White patriarchal representatives of the political future of the United States of America therefore quite logically constructed our model of a free democracy while at the same time institutionalizing slavery. The same logic allowed U.S. legislators many years later to exempt agricultural and domestic workers from minimum wage entitlements (Nordlund, 1977). Slaves, farm laborers, and domestic workers all work on and with the material foundations of life. They work with soil, and they attend to the dirt all bodies produce. They are the real bodies who do place-bound, physical work in and on the "natural," biological underground of life, their impurity has to be kept in check. They—and their exploitation—have to stay out of public sight, invisible, and private.

Developing a Coalitional Consciousness

Laura works ten hours a day as a *niñera*. She also volunteers at a workers' rights center where she organized a women's collective. Not all of its members are currently working as household workers, but all of them have firsthand knowledge of this work in their own homes. Some of them have also direct experience with the violent implications of patriarchal social relations enacted in private homes or home-workplaces. The women sometimes meet at the workers' center, other times in private homes. As a member of the collective, I regularly participate in their meetings.

When the women are among themselves, they talk freely and extensively. Often a speaker enters a zone of deeply felt pain or rage. They engage in consciousness-raising by sharing personal stories, listen to each other with keen interest and compassion, and discuss what they see as manifestations of injustice, exploitation, and abuse. They also share resistance stories, talk about actions performed in the cracks, interstices of power relations within which they are living and working.

Cricket Keating describes how feminist consciousness-raising was originally conceived as "a radical democratic practice" (2005, p. 87) that challenged the public/private divide, created transformative, non-hierarchical spaces, and linked theory and practice (p. 90). At the same time, its predominantly White middle-class participants tended to create a fictive unity of gender by considering the "me too" moment its "analytical heart," thereby excluding experiences of women of color. Keating proposes to instead place the development of connections among women divided by unequal social relations of power at the center of the process, thus changing it from consciousness-*raising* to one of *building a coalitional consciousness* (p. 94).

New Directions for Adult and Continuing Education • DOI: 10.1002/ace

In *Power Lines* Aimee Carrillo Rowe (2008) pursues a similar line of thought. Power lines are "conduits of the unevenness of modernity" created by centuries of colonial and neocolonial conquest and oppression (p. 2). However, they also "connect us to one another and to circuits of power" (p. 1), thus creating or maintaining relations of power.

Relations are not fixed, or "in place" like one's particular social location and related categorical identity. Relations are alive, they move, they shift, and they keep animating different perceptions, emotions, or value structures. This means that critically reflecting on one's social location and corresponding positionality is not enough when trying to build a coalitional consciousness. Engaging in reflective inquiry needs to be carried by the desire to connect with the world of others, to build "differential belongings" (Rowe, p. 179). Rowe emphasizes that this can only be done when adhering to a "politics of love," where "love" refers to its "more expansive sense of whose lives matter to us. Whose well-being is essential to our own" (p. 3). Her notion of a politics of love draws on Jean-Luc Nancy's writings (1991) who states that love "demands boundless generosity," asking us "not to choose between loves, not to privilege, not to hierarchize, not to exclude" (p. 82). According to Rowe, only such boundless generosity makes it possible to form an alliance, and to turn into "a set of relational unfolding" (2008, p. 51). In Cheval Sandoval's (2000) terms, a politics of love allows for building a "differential consciousness."

Building a differential consciousness is not simply a matter of opening our eyes, looking around, and perceiving others. Instead, it is a long and arduous process that is carried by a desire for creating differential belongings. This desire undergirds the courage required for investigating our individual lives, and our social identity in relation to many others that not only include those whose lives matter most to us, but above all those whose survival we must "overlook in order to connect to power in the ways we do" (Rowe, p. 3). In other words, we have to investigate how our categorical homes of race-ethnicity, culture, or gender have silently been participating in constructing those whose well-being we ignore even though our lives may depend on their existence. By laying bare these silent productions we excavate associated cherished "categorical belongings" (Rowe), and we see them as the discolored or deformed fragments that together represent the dominant order.

Excavating and getting rid of categorical belongings means moving to the outer edge of one's sense of self and "peering down into an abyss" (Rowe, p. 178). It is a lonely experience, but it is also embedded in a sense of self that always stands in relation, that wants to be able to relate differently and in multiple ways to the many whose lives our categorical belongings have left out, distorted, or violated. Looking down the abyss, questioning, or getting rid of one's essential belongings therefore means opening a space between "be" and "longing" (p. 178), a space that is ready to be filled with differential categorical belongings.

New Directions for Adult and Continuing Education • DOI: 10.1002/ace

As substitute mothers *niñeras* do motherwork, thus adding a key ingredient to the politics of love, one that neither Keating nor Rowe specifically address. Motherwork cannot ignore the physical, bodily, place-bound grounding of living beings, neither can our efforts of scrutinizing all our relations. We always need to include our relation to our physical facticity in our interrogations. We can only break the current of patriarchal thinking, interrupt and cut through patriarchal power lines by making our relation to the physical conditions of all life, our own included, an integral part of our investigative process.

This opens an important question concerning radically democratic learning. Does it change its parameters, its specificities, depending on where the learners find themselves, where they *categorically* place themselves in relation to our bodily facticity, and to the earth that carries and nourishes it? Are learning challenges or learning blocks stronger or weaker depending on how close or how far the learner is placed in relation to the lovers of purity?

Foreign household workers move about in the interstices of being "neither/nor, but kind of both, not quite either," of being "in the middle of either/or" (Lugones, 2003, p. 122). This in-between state submerges the workers in intense, painful, and often quite contradictory emotions. However, it also harbors resistive ways of seeing, living, and relating.

When making mayonnaise, oil, water, and yolk sometimes "curdle," that is, they don't blend well but coalesce more in the direction of one or the other, leaving one "with yolky oil or oily yolk" (Lugones, p. 122). Curdling illustrates a failed attempt of cleanly separating the pure from the impure. As a political metaphor curdling refers to the resistive potential of this failed attempt. When different oppressions "intermesh" rather than "interlock" (Lugones, p. 146), they curdle, thus leaving behind "segregated alliances" that keep intact related social fragmentations (Rowe, 2008, p. 177). In other words, curdling enacts its resistive quality by creating worlds within worlds, by blurring the boundary markers that separate, keep apart.

Caring for someone's children can only be performed in a state of curdling, a state already implied by the very term "substitute mothers." Substitute mothers creatively occupy a space that is not theirs to give loving care to a stranger's child. Doing care work in a home that is crisscrossed by cultural and patriarchal demarcations and lines of separation therefore means receiving intense training in making vital epistemological and ethical shifts that allow to see, love, and care across profound differences. The workers creatively and lovingly resist social fragmentations. They practice, embody the politics of love.

Their learning challenges are therefore fundamentally different from those "parading as pure" (Lugones, 2003, p. 130). Household workers face the challenge of undoing their sense of powerlessness and inferiority, of finding their voice, and of claiming their rights. Those who have the power to keep household work out of public sight by delegating it to the impure,

New Directions for Adult and Continuing Education • DOI: 10.1002/ace

that is, to those seen most fit for doing it, face a different challenge. They need to start the investigative process by questioning this very move, and how and why the workers' lives do not matter to them, are as irrelevant as the work they do. They need to start seeing both their actual as well as their categorical home "as a place never before seen" (Rowe, 2008, p. 55).

Breaking the Circuit of Patriarchal Power Lines

None of the various community-based labor and immigration advocacy groups I contacted address the particular struggles of domestic workers. This large and growing working population was even more strikingly absent in a conference for "engaged scholars" on migration and low-wage work (Low-Wage Work, Migration and Gender Conference, University of Illinois, Chicago, March 13–14, 2008). A workshop one of the Latino staff members of the workers' rights center regularly offers does not mention issues relating to domestic work, nor are they addressed in any of the center's brochures and fact sheets.

When Laura and I organized an educational event on domestic workers' labor rights, none of the staff members attended. On the big calendar on the wall of the center's office the event was marked as "women's group meeting." I asked the director why this was not announced as a workshop on the labor rights of domestic workers, especially because the staff knew little or nothing about them. He responded by emphasizing that he and his staff are very sensitive toward "gender issues." In other words, he trafficked in the political correctness of gender sensitivity, thereby erasing the women as workers. In a later discussion of a grant proposal I had submitted to my university the director did not like the budget item relating to renting a room for the collective. He emphasized that the women already had such a place because they could freely enter the center's multiuse office space during its hours of operation. I asked him whether he had ever heard of Virginia Woolf's A Room of One's Own. He became very upset and ended the discussion. In other words, even a hint of feminism threatened his gender sensitivity that he needed to keep safely within patriarchal, head-of-household parameters.

The examples given above illustrate that the circuits of patriarchal power lines are strong and omnipresent, even in the minds of those claiming to be allies. Where categorical belongings construct privileges built on silences and patriarchal dismissals of vital work and experiences, moving to the edge of one's self not only means letting go of one's cherished identities but also facing the momentary terror of letting go of some of one's most taken-for-granted privileges. In other words, without any willingness to confront this abyss, a rather rock-solid, seemingly unmovable learning block cannot be set in motion to roll away.

Based on my experiences and observations regarding the labor struggles of immigrant household workers, this willingness can indeed be fostered and eventually can turn into the "heartfelt grappling" with the conditions of privilege (Rowe, 2008, p. 54) when it is embedded in a coalitional political space, one created by the household workers themselves. Where patriarchal power lines crisscross with others, and where those excluded from them have already developed their voice, are speaking loudly, and are claiming their rights, the lovers of purity are continuously being reminded of the importance of unlearning their patriarchal sense of power and entitlement. Only such unlearning can open a space for the political voices that call for the recognition and validation of household labor, and of what it represents in the web of social relations.

Building Political Alliances

As a member of the collective, I have been involved in many conversations about the tremendous obstacles caused by the patriarchal dismissals of women's work. We sought out and met with representatives of women's organizations and community-based labor advocacy groups who were open to developing a more differential understanding of related struggles. Finally, four of us traveled to California and participated in a regional conference organized by members of the National Alliance of Household Workers. There I observed quite different kinds of learning challenges, how participants called attention to them, and how they were consciously addressed via a number of different learning modalities.

The march of immigrant and native household workers and their allies through San Francisco made them visible as workers with unique labor struggles. By walking the streets with banners, songs, and shouts they defied the public–private division, and thus the geography of domination. Moreover, the mix of genders, ages, colors, racial-ethnic markers, and languages not only signified the global dimension of immigrant household labor but also the coalitional nature of their struggle.

The march was followed by two days of workshops. They were conducted in a consciously created, lively coalitional space that brought together multiple social realities, but all under the banner of validating household work and strengthening the political organization of household workers. Male community organizers clearly had to face different challenges than white academic women, as did women of color who not only were proudly claiming their voice, but had to also acknowledge the efforts of their White or male allies.

Some of the workshops provided important information about a variety of issues, such as the toxicity of cleaning chemicals, the history of domestic workers in the United States, or immigration reform. Some also offered different kinds of training where the participants discussed and practiced, for instance, ways of negotiating with an employer, or of responding to an employer's racism. Experiences of injustice at the workplace were narrated or acted out through storytelling and role-playing. The participants were guided through practicing responses that fostered their self-worth and sense of power.

The majority of workers were women of color. The White participants were mostly students, representatives of unions, or academic-activists like me. We came as allies, but we were also clearly reminded of the many challenges we have to confront to be able to engage in deep coalitions with the workers. For instance, patriarchal blinders were challenged in a workshop on labor history that exclusively focused on union struggles, thereby once again excluding household workers who by federal law are prevented from forming unions. Class privilege was called into question in a workshop on socially engaged research where a household worker challenged the middle-class academic participants to not just utilize or flaunt their institutional class-based power. Their angry criticism required the researchers to redefine their access to institutional power as a "bridge to power," turning it into a useful resource, one that unequivocally benefits those categorically excluded from it (Rowe, 2008, p. 180).

The various activities and events happening at the conference enacted all the core ingredients of radically democratic learning I previously discussed. They illustrated the vital importance of forming alliances by engaging in the long and strenuous effort of building a coalitional consciousness.

The Spiral of Radically Democratic Learning

As discussed in this chapter, certain experiences propel whereas others block radically democratic learning. Those that propel are also those that need to break through the social walls of disinterest or invisibility. They need to become palpably, audibly, bodily present. Due to the thoroughly entrenched, omnipresent nature of patriarchal-colonialist value structures, this is the most radical aspect of democratic learning, one that interrogates the deep structure of capitalist patriarchy. What makes such learning democratic is the desire mentally and spiritually to let different kinds of oppressions, be they cultural, class-based, sexual, racial, ethnic, or bodily curdle in one's heart and understanding, to engage in "a politics of becoming" that allows the "fluidity of movement across communities" (Rowe, 2008, pp. 177, 179).

Small children and their immigrant substitute mothers live the possibility of creating worlds within worlds, of undoing the hard-edged social fragmentation of a power-based, unjust, and life-destroying system. Children respond to the care of their *niñera*. They love her. Her skin color means nothing to them, nor does her accent, her immigrant status, her class. As long as they feel cared for, loved, and protected they cross lines of separation with remarkable ease. Love and protection include, however, the children's physical growth and well-being. A theory of radically democratic learning therefore cannot bypass the material, the biological, the physical.

New Directions for Adult and Continuing Education • DOI: 10.1002/ace

Otherwise it would simply build attractive conceptual structures, parading as pure by floating above the impure, the bodily.

Radically democratic learning is not a linear process that starts with a critical reflection on an unjust system and where one is placed in it, possibly followed by testing one's newly gained insights in one's daily practices and encounters. Rather, the learners keep distancing themselves from, and are moving closer to a number of recurring points, each time creating a new loop in a growing and widening spiral. For instance, they move closer to, or away from, and closer again, to critique and affirmation, insight and on-the-ground practice, separation, and connection. Each learner starts at a different point of these spiral moves, but shares with others a longing, a yearning for community that is rooted in a collective sense of self, of being in relation with all living and nonliving things on earth. Being in relation means being responsible for caring, maintaining, and protecting life and its conditions. Without such a collective sense of self there is no longing for relating and protecting, radically democratic learning cannot take place, and fundamental social changes will not happen. There will be no life after democracy.

References

Bauman, W. "Essentialism, Universalism, and Violence: Unpacking the Ideology of Patriarchy." *Journal of Women and Religion,* 2003, *19/20*(1), 52–71.

Hart, M. "Women, Migration, and the Body-Less Spirit of Patriarchal Capitalism." *Journal of International Women's Studies,* 2005, 7(2). Retrieved February 6, 2010, from http://www.bridgew.edu/SoAS/jiws/Nov05V2/Hart.pdf

Keating. C. "Building Coalitional Consciousness. *National Women's Studies Association Journal,* 2005, 17(2), 86–103.

Klein, R. "The Politics of Cyberfeminism: If I'm a Cyborg Rather Than a Goddess Will Patriarchy Go Away?" In S. Hawthorne and R. Klein (eds.), *Cyberfeminism: Connectivity, Critique and Creativity* (pp. 185–212). North Melbourne: Spinifex Press, 1999.

Lugones, M. *Pilgrimages/Peregrinajes: Theorizing Coalition Against Multiple Oppressions.* Lanham, Md.: Rowman & Littlefield, 2003.

Nancy, J.-L. *The Inoperative Community.* Minneapolis: University of Minnesota Press, 1991.

Nordlund, J. W. *The Quest for a Living Wage: The History of the Federal Minimum Wage Program.* Westport, Conn.: Greenwood Press, 1977.

Roy, A. "Democracy's Falling Light." *Outlook India Magazine,* July 13, 2009. Retrieved July 15, 2009, from http://www.outlookindia.com/article.aspx?250418.

Rowe, A. C. *Power Lines: On the Subject of Feminist Alliances.* Durham, N.C. and London: Duke University Press, 2008.

Sandoval, C. *Methodology of the Oppressed.* Minneapolis: University of Minnesota Press, 2000.

von Werlhof, C. "Losing Faith in Progress: Capitalist Patriarchy as an 'Alchemical System.'" In V. Bennholdt-Thomsen, N. Faraclas, and C. V. Werlhof (eds.), *There Is an Alternative: Subsistence and Worldwide Resistance to Corporate Globalization* (pp. 15–40). London and New York: Zed Books, 2001.

MECHTHILD HART *is a professor in the School for New Learning, DePaul University, Chicago.*

5

The author argues that worker education should facilitate both technical efficiency and high levels of worker participation and gives examples of how this can be done.

Productive and Participatory: Basic Education for High-Performing and Actively Engaged Workers

Paul Jurmo

The adult basic education field in the United States has experienced an ebb and flow of interest and investment in "worker education" over the past three decades. Although the rhetoric around workplace basic skills tends to focus on such outcomes as productivity and competitiveness, some proponents of worker basic education see it as a tool for democratizing U.S. workplaces.

But efforts to use employee education to increase worker control, responsibility, and reward vis-à-vis workplace operations have been hindered by inadequate coordination; lack of sustained, accessible funding; and limited evaluation, documentation, and dissemination of program models. Further complicating these efforts is an economy in which the notion of "democracy in the workplace" is often seen as a vestige of food coops, labor unions, Saturn auto plants, and other experiments at worker decision making and ownership dismissed by some as idealistic and unworkable.

But American workers, employers, educators, policy makers, and other stakeholders are now being challenged to think differently. We are being asked to rekindle the ingenuity and contribution of all workers, find new solutions to unemployment, be more competitive, and create a new kind of American economy. Those who are interested in creating economic models that rely on a highly engaged workforce can learn from the past three decades of worker-centered education. Advocates for worker education as a tool for both worker productivity and more democratic workplaces now have an opportunity to fill a leadership gap in the adult education and workforce development fields.

NEW DIRECTIONS FOR ADULT AND CONTINUING EDUCATION, no. 128, Winter 2010 © 2010 Wiley Periodicals, Inc.
Published online in Wiley Online Library (wileyonlinelibrary.com) • DOI: 10.1002/ace.390

47

This chapter summarizes how worker education programs have promoted "worker productivity" and "worker participation." It then suggests how advocates for democratic workplaces can develop a new model of worker basic education that enables workers to contribute to organizational efficiency while also participating at high levels of control, responsibility, and reward vis-à-vis their work.

In What Ways Do Workers "Participate"?

When discussing how adult basic education can serve U.S. workers, it is important to be clear about what a "worker" is. "Being a worker" can mean many things, depending on:

1. **Employment status.** Is the individual a job seeker, incumbent worker connected to one employer, a "free agent" (consultant/contractor) (Imel, 2001), or retiree (Stein, 2002)?
2. **Venue for participation.** Is the worker a job seeker trying to navigate the employment system external to a workplace? Is he or she an employee operating within a particular workplace owned by someone else? Or is the worker self-employed, operating within an organization owned by the employee and perhaps others?
3. **Level of participation.** At which of the following levels of participation is the worker operating?
    *   *Level 1: Nominal participation.* The worker is nominally present in the organization, doing part-time, contracted, and perhaps low-status and short-time work assignments with limited commitment by the worker and/or employer to an ongoing relationship.
    *   *Level 2: Actively following orders.* The worker is actively engaged in carrying out work procedures that are defined by others.
    *   *Level 3: Limited input in decision making.* The worker is given opportunities to give some input into how the organization is run, with final decisions made by others.
    *   *Level 4: High-level participation.* The worker has high levels of control, responsibility, and reward vis-à-vis the work. This is where what is sometimes referred to as "workplace democracy" can occur.

What Do Workers Need to Participate at High Levels?

To attain, retain, and participate effectively in a job, a worker needs both "career tools" and external supports.

Career Tools. Career tools are the strengths/assets that the worker possesses (Jurmo, 2008), including:

*   *Transferable basic skills* such as the communication, decision-making, interpersonal, and lifelong learning skills defined by the *Equipped for the Future Standards* (Stein, 2000)

New Directions for Adult and Continuing Education • DOI: 10.1002/ace

- *Other technical and cultural knowledge and skills* required to navigate particular work systems
- *Self-efficacy* (a belief that one can achieve something valuable through effort; Brown, 1999a)
- *Credentials* (academic, occupational, legal) required for employment (Brown, 1999b)
- *A career and education plan* (Comings, Parrella, and Soricone, 2000; Wonacott, 2002)

External Supports. External supports are found in the various institutions within which the worker functions. These supports are necessary if the worker is to be able to apply the above-described career tools to get to work each day and participate actively and productively in that workplace. Workers need to be able to manage housing, food, clothing, transportation, healthcare, childcare, and eldercare responsibilities if they are to be able to get to work. These personal supports are typically provided through collaboration with family members and/or other institutions. At the workplace, a worker needs to have tools, equipment, and a safe environment, as well as moral support, guidance, and efficient work procedures provided by employers, co-workers, and perhaps a labor union. Workers also need to be rewarded financially, with appropriate pay and benefits.

To participate at higher levels (Levels 3 and 4 above) within a workplace, workers not only need the above basic internal career tools and external supports, but additional special tools and supports, as well. These include:

- *Leadership skills* (e.g., critical thinking, teamwork, decision-making, conflict resolution, planning) and high levels of productivity skills (i.e., a strong ability to carry out the technical requirements of the work)
- *A work environment that provides opportunities and incentives* for workers to participate at high levels

How Has Adult Basic Education Been Used to Prepare U.S. Adults for Work?

Historically, most adult basic education programs have focused at least in part on the goal of helping participants prepare for the world of work. They do this in response to funder requirements, but also because most people who come to these programs are motivated by work-related goals: to get a job, perform a current job better and/or more comfortably, and prepare for career advancement. Many adult education programs use generic basic skills curricula to help their learners achieve their work-related goals on the grounds that these curricula help adults (1) develop portable basic skills they can use in any work-related task, and/or (2) earn the general equivalency diploma (GED) that they need to move into better jobs and further education (Jurmo, 2004).

In the 1980s and early 1990s, there was a spurt in interest in creating special programs that focused specifically on work-related basic skills. Workplace literacy initiatives were established at national levels by federal agencies, trade associations, and labor unions, and at the state level (Jurmo, 1996). Special curricula (usually variations on contextualized approaches) and program models were developed, to engage employers and unions in establishing worker basic skills programs to enhance worker productivity, their ability to handle new work and safety procedures and technologies, and maintain job security, while helping employers to stay competitive in a new global economy. The language surrounding these efforts tended to emphasize employer goals like "enhancing worker productivity" and "building business competitiveness." However, some voices argued for an alternative, "worker-centered" view of worker basic education (see next section). Although considerable work was done from the mid-1980s to mid-1990s to build workplace education models, support from federal and state agencies, employers, and labor unions declined significantly from the latter 1990s to today (Imel, 2003; Jurmo, 1998b; Rosen, 2008).

Although the above workplace education initiatives focused primarily on the skills of incumbent (already employed) workers, from the early 1990s to today there has also been a fluctuating interest in how to ensure that unemployed out-of-school youth and adults are prepared to move into work. Every few years a new national report has stated that school-aged youth or various adult populations are not ready for the new U.S. workforce (Commission on the Skills of the American Workforce, 1990, 2006; Johnston and Packer, 1987; National Commission on Adult Literacy, 2008; Venezky, Kaestle, and Sum, 1987). Most of these reports have argued for the kinds of contextualized learning approaches that were developed in the workplace basic education initiatives described above (Center for Law and Social Policy, 2009; Maguire, Freely, Clymer, and Conway, 2009; Wrigley, Richer, Martinson, Kubo, and Strawn, 2003).

How Have Adult Educators Focused on Helping U.S. Workers Participate at Higher Levels?

Although much of the workplace education rhetoric focused on the need to upgrade workers' basic skills for the sake of organizational productivity and competitiveness, there were a number of national, state, and local adult basic education initiatives aimed at helping workers participate at high levels of control, responsibility, and reward vis-à-vis their work. These efforts were largely carried out by (1) adult education professionals who were guided by participatory, learner-centered principles of adult learning, and/or (2) workplace education professionals who wished to promote collaborative workplaces, workplace democracy, and/or social justice.

Proponents of what was sometimes called a "worker-centered" perspective questioned assumptions about worker basic education being circulated by the media and policy makers (Jurmo, 1994; Working for America Institute, 1999). "Worker-centered" proponents argued, for example, that the mainstream viewpoint too heavily favored employer interests and neglected workers' (Harris, 2000), focused too heavily on training workers for immediate and/or narrow tasks rather than preparing them for longer-term success and advancement in a variety of jobs (Gowen, 1992), did not reflect the actual skill demands of U.S. jobs (Hull, 1993), and in some cases denigrated workers' abilities (Schultz, 1992) or reduced workers to resources to be manipulated (Schied, 2001).

"Worker-centered" advocates made the case that workers need to be respected for their abilities and contributions and able to protect their self-interests in workplaces and an economy that presented a number of threats to worker well-being (Hull, 1997). These threats included significant job insecurity and reduced wages and benefits as jobs disappeared, were reconfigured, or lost protections historically provided by employers, unions, and government policies (Sarmiento, 2001). To deal with these challenges, workers needed skills and knowledge to

- *Protect themselves against unfair labor practices in their places of work*: Workers need particular skills to be able to protect themselves against discrimination (by age, race, gender, disability, sexual orientation) and unsafe working conditions, unfair wage and benefit policies, and inappropriate work requirements. This self-protection can include being able to participate in a labor union.
- *Respond to changing working conditions and pursue new job opportunities within their companies,* while ensuring that they retain appropriate wages, benefits, and rights
- *Protect themselves in the event of layoff,* by creating effective career plans, navigating unemployment systems, and otherwise taking action to secure meaningful, rewarding employment
- *Participate in decisions* regarding workplace practices and/or policies
- *Create and operate their own businesses*
- *Prepare for and succeed in retirement*

Drawing on these worker-centered arguments, adult educators created programs designed to help workers meet the above goals. Many of these programs also focused on employer goals, on the grounds that for companies and workers to survive in a competitive economy, both stakeholder groups need to be supported (Working for America Institute, 2001). Examples are described below.

Curriculum Frameworks and Models. The Equipped for the Future (EFF) Systems Reform Initiative (Spangenberg and Watson, 2003) advocated for the reforming of the U.S. adult basic education system.

EFF expanded the concept of "basic skills" to include problem-solving, teamwork, planning, research, self-advocacy, conflict-resolution, and other key skills that workers need to participate actively in the job search process and in the workplace. EFF proposed the use of contextualized educational practices, which focus instruction on real-world uses of basic skills relevant to learners. These practices would maximize learning efficiency and help learners see learning as a tool for achieving personally meaningful goals. EFF also argued that administrators, policy makers, and funders need to create an infrastructure to support this work and thereby develop a more rational system of adult basic education.

Problem-Posing at Work: Some workplace education programs pushed participants to move beyond solving of problems defined by others to "problem posing" (as defined by Paulo Freire, 1970). In this approach, workers are invited to identify problems in their workplaces, analyze contributing factors, identify potential solutions, and—in some cases—present their findings to supervisors. In upstate New York, employees at several manufacturing sites worked in teams to present recommendations to management for improving workplace operations (Jurmo, 1998a). In a company-sponsored employee education program at a corporate headquarters in New York City, mailroom staff analyzed how the conveyor system that delivered mail could be improved (author research). In California in the 1980s, an instructor helped immigrant employees develop English skills by taking photos of various artifacts in the worksite (e.g., safety equipment) and using them to trigger theme-based discussion of workplace issues (Añorve, 1989).

Understanding and Protecting Worker Rights: A number of programs (Wallerstein and Auerbach, 1987) help workers understand and protect their rights as workers. In one example from the University of Massachusetts Labor Extension Program (2003), participants learn about "Your Pay and Your Paycheck," "Rights of Workers Under Eighteen," "Protection from Discrimination," and "Unions and the Right to Organize."

Reflecting on Workplace Issues: In New England, adult educators engaged learners in research about the work histories of their family members; the hourly wage; "women's work"; the challenges of balancing work and family life; unions, using the film *Norma Rae* in the classroom; homophobia, racism, and sexual harassment in the workplace; immigrants in the U.S. workplace; and workplace safety (New England Literacy Resource Center, 1998).

Work-Readiness Curricula: Several "work-readiness" curricula (Equipped for the Future National Center, 2006) adapt the Equipped for the Future standards and focus in particular on problem-solving skills needed in a variety of workplace settings, including healthcare (Industry-Business Institute, 2009a) and the transportation/logistics/distribution industry (Industry-Business Institute, 2009b).

Financial Literacy for Working Adults: Some financial literacy programs have been developed on the premise that adults not only need to be able to attain and retain employment and thereby earn income and benefits; workers also need to be able to manage their income and benefits in smart ways. In Albany, New York, community college instructors worked with a company's human resources department to help employees to understand and efficiently manage the financial (e.g., investment plans), health, and vacation benefits available to them. The company saw this as a way to not only help employees maximize these benefits but to reduce the demands that workers were placing on human resources staff when they came asking for information, did not fill out forms correctly, or otherwise failed to perform the tasks that the new benefits packages required of workers (Jurmo, 1998a).

Protecting Worker Health and Safety: Some curricula help lower-skilled adults maintain their health by learning about diet, exercise, stress management, risk avoidance, and dealing with healthcare providers and health insurance plans. Some programs also focus on how to avoid and deal with particular workplace hazards, including repetitive stress injuries, poor ergonomics, toxins, falls, fires, noise, eye injuries, and workplace violence. These programs argue that, for workers to be able to get a job, retain it, attend regularly, and avoid injury, they need to know how to maintain their health and safety (Utech, 2005).

Leadership Development for Adult Learners: "Adult learner leadership" has been promoted by a national adult learner organization, several state-level learner groups, and at the program level within the adult literacy field. This is done through leadership training (at conferences and workshops), hiring of learners as staff, and creation of roles for learners on program boards and committees and as advocates and spokespersons. Advocates argue that, by practicing leadership skills within the supportive environment of an education program, learners are then prepared to transfer those skills to their roles in the workplace, family, and community.

Career and Educational Planning: Some curricula help job seekers (unemployed individuals or incumbent workers who want to move into new positions) to develop career and educational plans. Learners identify career goals, explore career options, identify target jobs to pursue, decide how they will manage personal responsibilities (e.g., childcare, transportation, housing, manage personal finances, further education) that must be dealt with to successfully hold a job, prepare a plan for moving ahead to pursue a job, prepare a resume and cover letter, get ready for job interviews, and establish an ongoing support system (Colette, Woliver, Bingman, and Merrifield, 1996; Industry-Business Institute, 2009c; Oesch and Bouer, 2009; Women Employed, 2008).

Other Ways That Adult Education Programs Help Learners Prepare for High Levels of Workplace Participation. In addition to using instruction, adult education programs help learners for active roles in the workplace by

- *Creating leadership roles for learners* within the program, as staff members, members of boards and committees, and as spokespersons and advocates
- *Providing a safe and positive environment* where participants can try on new roles, meet new people, rethink who they are and what they want to achieve, fail and try again, and learn from the examples provided by staff and fellow students
- *Helping learners get access to support services* (e.g., income, childcare, housing), which provide the practical and emotional supports they need to get a job and perform it with confidence

What Advocates Can Do to Build a "Productivity through Participation" Approach

At a time when the need for a well-educated workforce continues to grow, those who see worker education as a tool for both worker productivity and more democratic workplaces now have an opportunity to fill a leadership gap in the field.

Outlined below are actions that advocates for a "productivity through participation" approach to worker basic education can take.

Rethink the model. In the past three decades, there has been a tendency to reduce the arguments for worker basic education into two camps: those who favor an employer-oriented approach (emphasizing worker productivity and company competitiveness) and those who promote a worker-centered perspective (that stresses quality of work life—including job security and meaningful roles—for workers). Rather than see these as mutually exclusive goals, advocates for a worker-centered perspective might argue that both sets of goals must be achieved if companies are to survive and thrive and if workers are to stay employed and advance.

Build systems that adapt effective practices. There is a big tendency in the work-related basic education field to not learn from experience and research, to continually rediscover the worker basic skills issue, and to reinvent educational practices. The field thus never advances very far. Policy makers and practitioners should all take the time to learn from past experience, agree on guidelines for effective practice, and then continually refine those guidelines and associated practices.

Advocate for quality. At all levels—at the policy and funding level and within programs—practitioners need to continually advocate for effective practices and resist the urge to "just settle" for what we can get.

Persevere. Though workforce basic education has often been marginalized, we all need to persevere and remember that this work is vital to the building of a more productive and just economy.

References

Añorve, R. "Community-Based Literacy Educators: Experts and Catalysts for Change." In A. Fingeret and P. Jurmo (eds.), *Participatory Literacy Education*. New Directions for Continuing Education, no. 42 (pp. 35–42). San Francisco: Jossey-Bass, 1989.

Brown, B. L. "Self-Efficacy Belief and Career Development." ERIC Digest 205. Columbus, Ohio: ERIC Clearinghouse, 1999a.

Brown, B. L. "Vocational Certificates and College Degrees." ERIC Digest 212. Columbus, Ohio: ERIC Clearinghouse, 1999b.

Center for Law and Social Policy. *Recommendations to Refocus WIA Title II on Career and Postsecondary Success*. Washington, D.C.: Center for Law and Social Policy, 2009.

Colette, M., Woliver, B., Bingman, M. B., and Merrifield, J. *Getting There: A Curriculum for Moving People into Employment* (ED413477). Knoxville: University of Tennessee, Center for Literacy Studies, 1996.

Comings, J., Parrella, A., and Soricone, L. "Helping Adults Persist: Four Supports." *Focus on Basics*, 2000, 4(A), 1–6.

Commission on the Skills of the American Workforce. *America's Choice: High Skills or Low Wages! The Report of the Commission on the Skills of the American Workforce*. Rochester, N.Y.: The National Center on Education and the Economy, 1990.

Commission on the Skills of the American Workforce. *Tough Choices or Tough Times*. Washington, D.C.: National Center on Education and the Economy, 2006.

Equipped for the Future National Center. Preparing for Work: An EFF Work Readiness Curriculum. Knoxville: University of Tennessee, Center for the Study of Adult Literacy, 2006.

Freire, P. *Pedagogy of the Oppressed*. New York: Herder and Herder, 1970.

Gowen, S. *The Politics of Workplace Literacy: A Case Study*. New York: Teachers College Press, 1992.

Harris, H. "Defining the Future or Reliving the Past? Unions, Employers, and the Challenge of Workplace Learning." Information Series 380. Columbus, Ohio: ERIC Clearinghouse, 2000.

Hull, G. "Hearing Other Voices: A Critical Assessment of Popular Views on Literacy and Work." *Harvard Educational Review*, 1993, 63(1), 20–49.

Hull, G. (ed.) *Changing Work, Changing Workers: Critical Perspectives on Language, Literacy, and Skills*. Albany: State University of New York Press, 1997.

Imel, S. "Career Development of Free Agent Workers." ERIC Digest 228. Columbus, Ohio: ERIC Clearinghouse, 2001.

Imel, S. "Whatever Happened to Workplace Literacy?" ERIC Myths and Realities 30. Columbus, Ohio: ERIC Clearinghouse, 2003.

Industry-Business Institute. *ESL for Healthcare Workers*. Elizabeth, N.J.: Union County College, 2009a.

Industry-Business Institute. *TLD Career Planning: Instructor's Guide*. Elizabeth, N.J.: Union County College, 2009.

Industry-Business Institute. *TLD Ready: Instructor's Guide*. Elizabeth, N.J.: Union County College, 2009b.

Johnston, W., and Packer, A. *Workforce 2000: Work and Workers for the 21st Century*. Indianapolis: Hudson Institute, 1987.

Jurmo, P. *Reinventing the NWLP: Recommendations for the National Workplace Literacy Program. A position paper submitted to the U.S. Department of Education in conjunction with the Reauthorization of the Adult Education Act*. Washington, D.C.: U.S. Department of Education, 1994.

Jurmo, P. *State Level Policy for Workplace Basic Education: What Advocates Are Saying*. Washington, D.C.: National Institute for Literacy, 1996.

Jurmo, P. *Collaborative Learning for Continuous Improvement: Team Learning and Problem Solving in a Workplace Education Program.* Albany: NY State Education Department, 1998a.

Jurmo, P. *Integrating Adult Basic Education with Workforce Development and Workplace Change: How National-Level Policy Makers Can Help.* Washington, D.C.: U.S. Department of Education, 1998b.

Jurmo, P. "Workplace Literacy Education: Definitions, Purposes, and Approaches." *Focus on Basics,* 2004, 7(B), 1–9.

Jurmo, P. *Creating a Workforce Learning System for Union County.* Elizabeth, N.J.: Union County College, 2008.

Maguire, S., Freely, J., Clymer, C., and Conway, M. *Job Training that Works: Findings from the Sectoral Employment Impact Study.* Vol. 7. New York: Public/Private Ventures, 2009.

National Commission on Adult Literacy. *Reach Higher, America: Overcoming Crisis in the U.S. Workforce.* New York: Council on the Advancement of Adult Literacy, 2008.

New England Literacy Resource Center. *The Changing World of Work. The Change Agent.* Boston: New England Literacy Resource Center, 1998.

Oesch, M., and Bouer, C. *Integrating Career Awareness into the ABE and ESOL Classroom.* Boston: National College Transitions Network, 2009.

Rosen, D. *International Workforce Literacy Review: United States.* New Zealand: Department of Labour, 2008.

Sarmiento, T. "Do Workplace Literacy Programs Promote High Skills or Low Wages? Suggestions for Future Evaluations of Workplace Literacy Programs." Labor Notes, a monthly newsletter of the Center for Policy Research of the National Governors Association, July 2001.

Schied, F. "Struggling to Learn, Learning to Struggle: Workers, Workplace Learning, and the Emergence of Human Resource Development." In V. Sheared and P. Sissel (eds.), *Making Space: Merging Theory and Practice in Adult Education* (pp. 124–137). Westport, Conn.: Bergin & Garvey, 2001.

Schultz, K. *Training for Basic Skills or Educating Workers? Changing Conceptions of Workplace Education Programs.* Berkeley: National Center for Research in Vocational Education, University of California, 1992.

Spangenberg, G., and Watson, S. *Equipped for the Future: Tools and Standards for Building and Assessing Quality Adult Literacy Programs.* New York: Council for the Advancement of Adult Literacy, 2003.

Stein, D. "The New Meaning of Retirement." ERIC Digest 215. Columbus, Ohio: ERIC Clearinghouse, 2002.

Stein, S. *Equipped for the Future Content Standards: What Adults Need to Know and Be Able to Do in the 21st Century.* Washington, D.C.: National Institute for Literacy, 2000.

University of Massachusetts Labor Extension Program. *The Boss Can't Do That, Can He? A Workers' Rights Curriculum.* Amherst: University of Massachusetts, 2003.

Utech, J. *Workplace Health and Safety ESOL Curriculum.* Amherst: Massachusetts Worker Education Roundtable, 2005.

Venezky, R., Kaestle, C., and Sum, A. *The Subtle Danger: Reflections on the Literacy Abilities of America's Young Adults.* Princeton, N.J.: Educational Testing Service, 1987.

Wallerstein, N., and Auerbach, E. *ESL for Action: Problem-Posing at Work.* Reading, Mass.: Addison-Wesley, 1987.

Women Employed. *Strategies for Success in Career Development: The Career Coach Curriculum Guide.* Chicago: Women Employed, 2008.

Wonacott, M. "Career Passports, Portfolios, and Certificates." ERIC Digest 238, Columbus, Ohio: ERIC Clearinghouse, 2002.

Working for America Institute. *Worker-Centered Learning: A Union Guide to Basic Skills.* Washington, D.C.: AFL-CIO, 1999.

Working for America Institute. *High Road Partnerships Report on Innovations in Building Good Jobs and Strong Communities.* Washington, D.C.: AFL-CIO, 2001.

Wrigley, H.S., Richer, E., Martinson, K., Kubo, H., and Strawn, J. *The Language of Opportunity: Expanding Employment Prospects for Adults with Limited English Skills.* Washington, D.C.: Center for Law and Social Policy, 2003.

PAUL JURMO is dean of economic development and continuing education at Union County College, Cranford, NJ.

6

In this chapter, three graduates and a faculty member analyze efforts to create a democratic practice in the context of their doctoral program in adult education.

Race, Power, and Democracy in the Graduate Classroom

Dianne Ramdeholl, Tania Giordani, Thomas Heaney, Wendy Yanow

A democratic tradition in adult education finds historical roots in the writings of Eduard Lindeman (1961), for whom adult education was essential to America's fledgling democracy. It is through education that people become informed and committed participants in decisions affecting their day-to-day lives. Democracy is self-government—government "of the people, by the people, and for the people."

Every human enterprise is governed, including graduate programs in adult education. To govern is to conduct the policies, actions, and affairs of that enterprise. But who governs a graduate classroom, how will the apparatus of government be formed, and whose interests will that government serve? These questions are at the core of any program preparing adult educators whose practice will support learner's participation in civil society. From its beginnings in 1996, the adult education doctoral program at National-Louis University (NLU; Chicago) encouraged both faculty and students to ask, "Who will govern? And how will a government be formed?"

Tensions and Contradictions

Higher education is not adult education. Despite faculty's attempt to import the best practices and principles of adult education into the classroom, there are systemic barriers to democracy in the academy. In traditional institutions of higher education, the answer to the first question is clear—faculty are assumed to govern the academic pursuits of the university, but the reality is experienced differently. How the government is formed is less uniformly

New Directions for Adult and Continuing Education, no. 128, Winter 2010 © 2010 Wiley Periodicals, Inc.
Published online in Wiley Online Library (wileyonlinelibrary.com) • DOI: 10.1002/ace.391

prescribed, but generally involves departments, committees, and academic officers in various combinations, but all putatively dominated by faculty. Although it is clear faculty are accountable for the integrity and academic quality of the university and, therefore, must have responsibility for governing programs and actions promoting learning and research, it is by no means clear that faculty alone bear this responsibility.

Democracy is a complex system of decision making that is too often uncritically embraced without acknowledging its complexity. What is it we mean by democracy in this chapter? We believe in the principle that people have a right to express their interests in decisions that affect them, but this is not to affirm anyone's right to prevail. We must ask of each decision, who is responsible (and thereby accountable) for the outcome? If special knowledge or expertise is demanded, who has this knowledge or expertise and by what means is this determined? When a decision has both harmful and beneficial consequences, who will weigh these effects and keep them in balance? There are decisions in which none of these questions are relevant, but there are many—and these tend to be the more critical decisions—in which they are.

In other words, participation in decision making, what we are calling democracy, is not inconsistent with authority—authority derived from responsibility, special knowledge or expertise, experience, or judicial wisdom. For example, academic decisions about the content of a field of study or the quality of academic performance, though open to the voice of learners, is ultimately the responsibility of faculty who are charged by the university and the professoriate to maintain high academic standards. At the same time, faculty has a responsibility to consider alternate views on curriculum, modes of discourse, and paradigms, whether these are presented by students or by peers.

The complexity of a democratic practice lies in the multiple roles we are called upon to play, depending on the nature of the decision to be made. At times we are advisory, at times we have direct jurisdiction, and at times we relinquish decisions to others. Monolithic views of democracy that insist on the equal participation of all are unworkable. The challenge is to sort through the array of agenda items on the planning table and to determine the appropriate response to each.

In attempting to build a democratic practice in the graduate classroom, we often lost sight of this complexity. Our participation was impacted by expectations, prior knowledge, expertise, time, effort, and a willingness to engage the process. How could our decision making be truly democratic when the loudest or most articulate voices often dominated? How could we hope to avoid the contaminants of dominant culture—competitiveness, self-interest, chauvinism—when these are deeply embedded in our lives?

Therefore, the challenge within our program began to take shape. How can students and faculty share the responsibility for governing? And how will they form a government? Each cohort in the NLU doctoral program has reflected on these questions. Faculty and students have written reflections on their experience (Baptiste, 2001; Baptiste and Brookfield, 1997; Bronte de Avila et al., 2001; Colin and Heaney, 2001). The following describes experiences of the fifth doctoral cohort (Doc5) as reported by three graduates and one member of the faculty.

Design and Seeds of Possibility

Doc5, a cohort of twenty-eight students, began their doctoral studies at a Summer Institute in 2004. Governance was presented at that institute as a space where students and faculty would share power. And its purpose was to provide a site for experiential learning related to democratic social change. Once a month during the fall and winter semesters and several times during the summer, the twenty-eight students would meet without faculty to discuss matters that could possibly affect the direction and richness of the program: curriculum, guest speakers, date by which to pick an advisor, support groups, teaching topics, and formats. Each semester, three students volunteered to serve as facilitator of these sessions; at the end of the meeting, faculty rejoined the group and one of the facilitators would make an oral report in front of the cohort and faculty about what the students had proposed. Usually the teaching team would approve, reject, or offer a compromise based on the request immediately.

In reflecting on seeds of possibility that were collectively sown by and among members of Doc5, the first Summer Institute provided initial, positive signs of a paradigmatic shift that never managed to reach full potential. There were signs of hope and goodwill, planted by students and faculty, which never blossomed into trees bearing fruit.

In retrospect, after lengthy reflection and discussion seems rather obvious, this was at the time outside our collective experiential and intellectual reach. We focused our attention on coming to understand, sometimes rather simplistically, often from the narrowness of an intellectual perspective, the meaning of democratic process. We developed our group understanding outside of a meaningful and complex understanding of power structures, which exist within racialized societies. Understanding racism was certainly, from a sociohistorical perspective, an essential component of the curriculum. Nevertheless, we did not address racism from an experiential perspective and we did not recognize the existence of racism, current and historical, as an essential understanding in the development of a democratic process.

Three Exemplifying Incidents. The discussions and growing understanding of both democracy and racism were taking place in parallel streams. The following three incidents outline some of the tensions and contradictions within this process of struggling toward democracy.

Choosing Advisors. Toward the end of their first year in the program, students had begun to identify their research topics—the fire in the belly that would sustain them through the rigors of a dissertation. The next step was to put together a committee of advisors who would guide their research over the next two years. To assure an equitable distribution of advising load, faculty had asked the cohort to set a date by which all requests for advisors would be made. Faculty wanted to review all requests before accepting any invitations.

Student governance met on the December weekend. For many students their choices for advisors were clear, but some needed more time to discuss their potential research topic with each of the faculty. There was growing momentum behind a January deadline, but a consensus proved impossible when Denise told the group that she could not make a decision that quickly. Suddenly, within what seemed to be a matter of seconds, a host of volatile emotions erupted. Members of the group argued that Denise was putting her own interests above those of her colleagues, thereby exercising White privilege. Others saw Denise as a victim, as a seemingly minor incident became intensely divisive. The weekend ended with anger, frustration, and accusations of privilege and racism.

Passing the Torch. A new cohort was to begin in the summer of 2006, so a subcommittee of Student Governance formed a welcoming committee. As part of this welcome the subcommittee asked each member of the cohort to write down one or two things they wished they had known about the program that would have helped them make more informed decisions on entry. The responses, made anonymously, were compiled and distributed to all students for revisions and additions.

During the next session of governance, one student argued that some of the statements were racist and needed to be eliminated. One statement, for example, pointed to "a heavy Africentric reading load" and added that "all curriculum selected is at the exclusion of other curriculum." Another statement read (ironically, in the light of the accusation of racism), "This program may change your life. It does not tolerate racism."

The ensuing discussion was heated and focused more on whether the group had the right to exclude anyone's statement than on the substance of the statements themselves. The reluctance of some to silence any individual was countered by charges of repressive tolerance. The meeting grew increasingly tense. Some argued that anyone who knowingly protected the identities of the authors of these statements were themselves complicit in racism. Others believed the words were not representative of the cohort and did not want their names associated with the document. In the midst of this contentious exchange, a significant number of students remained silent.

Teachable Moments Lost. The third incident speaks to the ways incidents and misunderstandings had been piling up on top of each other, destroying residual feelings of community and good will that marked the beginning of the doctoral program. By the third (and last) summer institute, the atmosphere was fraught with tension. At this point, many students felt their perspectives had been marginalized.

During the April weekend prior to the last Summer Institute, a White faculty member was asked the date by which that residential session would end. She was not scheduled to teach at the institute, but provided a date that, as events unfolded, turned out to be incorrect. Unfortunately, some students made commitments based on this inaccurate information.

A few weeks before the institute, another faculty member who was African American and was on the teaching team for the summer sent the cohort an e-mail indicating the session would end a day later than the date given in April. Some students responded to the e-mail angrily, saying commitments had already been made and they were not going to stay for that last day. Others thought this response was disrespectful to faculty. A flurry of contentious e-mails ensued over a student-only listserv—a mailing list that did not include faculty. At one point, an e-mail was sent with a black fist at the end—the symbol used by the Black Power Movement in the sixties. There emerged differing accounts of this student's intent.

Because faculty had not been included in this exchange of e-mails, no response from faculty was able to assuage the rising conflict. Many students avoided the fray, fearful of being scorched. Students arrived at the final institute filled with apprehension. One faculty member, who was now apprised of all that had transpired, encouraged the cohort to focus on tasks at hand, look forward, and not dwell on the contentious online exchange. Yet students spoke of little else. During governance they were tense and disengaged. At one point, some began counting off the number of sessions left to graduation, preferring to focus on their research. Eight students raised their hands, expressing a desire to collectively grapple with this latest attack on group solidarity, but they were in the minority. Resolution and healing never occurred.

What Do These Incidents Mean?

There was, in these incidents, an absence of shared vision of how society is constructed when people disagree. This difference in vision often results in conflict and misunderstandings. Some shared a philosophy that viewed adult education as a human rights struggle—a vision of constructing a world more equitable and just. Such a vision has the capacity to unite in concrete ways when differences threaten to divide. Others, however, were motivated more by self-interest than collective civic responsibility.

As a cohort, the majority of students were not struggling together for sustained periods in deep, fiery ways that bound the cohort together. Painful issues such as the three incidents were unresolved by the end of the term and often remained that way throughout the program. Although these issues might have seemed outwardly forgotten, they remained in many students' consciousness like cuts that never really healed.

The Summer Institute of 2004 was our first prolonged time together. Governance was a new outfit students were collectively trying on, there were enthusiastic discussions of forming different committees, such as a curriculum committee, as well as plans of different possible formats of disseminating information to the entire cohort. However, there seemed to be a general uncertainty of direction. Some students pointed out faculty's expertise and many felt they were too unfamiliar with the concepts to suggest adapting them. Because no explicit parameters were provided and no current examples of truly democratic societies to refer to, all experiences with this endeavor were limited. Students struggled to discern where the locus of power was, whether it ever left the faculty in significant or meaningful ways.

The conditions under which we live—the place where truths and realities are manipulated—support us living in a state of false consciousness (Brookfield, 2005). It didn't feel possible to even discern what people's authentic feelings were or what they thought they ought to be feeling. There was no critical analysis as an entire cohort to unpack the ugly exchanges that interrupted our meetings. Although there were attempts to make space to address some of these incidents, it was not enough. Did people feel supported/engaged enough to grapple with what was happening? Did faculty understand the complexity and charged nature of the space we were operating in? In retrospect, it seemed as if there needed to be space and commitment to sort through and analyze the "group think" to engage in meaningful consciousness-raising.

What's the Deeper Meaning?

In the end, it is a mistake to consider what happened in these incidents from any single critical lens. The experience was simply too complex and any useful analysis would require, as one of our faculty would suggest, a "layered analysis." And we would add to that layered analysis a spiraled one. We needed to look deep, but we also needed to go back and look again and again as our understanding grew. To look at this study solely from the standpoint of race or racism, which would not be difficult to do given the scenarios, at the very least, ignores the necessity to acknowledge the significance of power within the cohort. It is too easy to suggest that what was going on was a reflection of White privilege or racism or a duplication of power structures reflecting the dominant culture—even though that was certainly true. After all, this program was designed to focus upon issues of social justice. Applicants were accepted, in part, on the basis of their interest in concepts, theories, and actions that would challenge the status quo, certainly not strengthen it. So, it makes little sense to be narrow in our immediate analysis of this conflict as one singularly reflecting racism and/or another example of how the dominant culture insinuates itself into every aspect of our lives.

It seems, in considering the situation as a whole, much of the conflict and strife identified in these incidents seemed to begin with a profound and fundamental dysfunction resulting from a reaction to a feeling of power-lessness among all students. Ironically, at the same time, although we were in serious debate and study of Critical Theory, there was no recognition of the omnipresence of power and how that power was being acted upon. We did not understand racism as a manifestation of power. And we certainly did not recognize, given the omnipresence of power, how it is acted upon may or may not reflect traditionally dominant power structures. And when the manner in which power is acted upon reflects power structures in ways that challenge societal norms, a negative response to it can mask underlying power structures, the manifestations of which are often racism. Introducing students to Africentrism, for example, may have posed a threat to dominant power structures as some students embraced new understanding and feeling.

Employing the Critical Race Theory methodology of stories and counter-stories can help to illuminate our understanding of these scenarios. Even though the stories represented here do not necessarily offer all the points and counterpoints, our analysis recognizes that any story told comes from a socially constructed point of view (Delgado, 1989; Delgado and Stefancic, 2000). Therefore, a suggestion that the conflicts began as a reaction to our collective lack of power reflects a conclusion that ultimately supports the dominant position of color-blindness and White privilege. The suggestion that race may not be the vortex of the problem can also be understood as a suggestion of privilege. All experience we have must be considered from a historical as well as a sociocultural context. As a nation, we accepted the notion that we were a color-blind society. That acceptance disempowered the historical experiences of people of color (Dixson and Rousseau, 2006). When some students of color suggested that, when Denise stalled the process of selecting advisors, White privilege was at the core of understanding the issue, who is to argue with that? And, when it was White students who suggested that they would not be able to change their work schedules to remain another day at the summer institute, their perceived disrespect of an African-American faculty member warranted the Black Power Fist. Were those scenarios a function of White privilege? From a perpetrator perspective, race was not ever considered in the responses of the White students and so could not be the issue, but then that response came from students who lacked the historical or sociocultural experience of being of color. Color-blindness is a manifestation of power when it disempowers historical experiences. The question is about more than what was intentionally done, it was also about how what happened may have felt to some students of color (Freeman, 1977–1978).

Where Do We Go from Here?

Democracy is built on the promise of equality. Racism and perceptions of racism are viral enemies of democratic practice. Incivility and occasional violence have recently invaded the political scene from town hall meetings to the chambers of Congress. Few civil-minded Americans welcome the mention of race as an underlying factor in the virulent public debates over healthcare reform or responses to the financial crisis, but former President Jimmy Carter has raised the question. Speaking of Representative Joe Wilson's outburst during President Barack Obama's address to Congress, Carter said Wilson's comments were "based on racism" (Grossman, 2009). Carter's statement gave voice to many who viewed Wilson in the context of all vitriolic speech permeating political discourse over the past months. Nonetheless, that statement was rejected by many who believed it tantamount to saying all criticism of an African-American president is racist.

At issue is the subtlety with which race enters our discourse. When Joe Wilson cried out, "You lie!" to the president during a joint session of Congress, the words themselves made no reference to race (Nicholas and Simon, 2009). By what logic, therefore, can a reasonable person conclude that these words were "based on racism"? A core concept of Critical Race Theory can help us understand this: microaggressions—"subtle insults (verbal, nonverbal, and/or visual) directed at people of color, often automatically or unconsciously" (Solórzano, Ceja, and Yosso, 2000, p. 60). The impact of these insults is cumulative. Patterns of behavior emerge over time that no longer disguise an underlying racist intent. In the three incidents from Governance described above, a reader could well conclude that it was far from clear that the dysfunctions were caused by racism, although perceptions of racism were clearly present. The fact is that disruptions occur in response to events that conclude a chain of events that might have begun in a forgotten past. Perceptions of racism reflect on patterns of behavior only partially present. They are reality for those who experience them. Moreover, those perceptions reflect the omnipresence of power and privilege that are rarely recognized and even less often acknowledged.

As we have seen in the incidents of governance, we cannot engage in a democratic practice when racism and perceptions of racism invade the forum in which decisions are to be made. Democracy requires an antiracist stance, which in turn requires a recognition of the existence of traditionally dominant power structures, many of which emanated from a racist ideology. There is irony in the fact that the graduate program discussed here has a curriculum infused with Africentric, Africanist, and Critical Race Theories, Racial Identity Theory, White Privilege, and is built on literature reflecting multiple racial, cultural, and ethnic perspectives. This curriculum is obviously not enough. Although immersion in the historic and academic discourse of race is critical to an antiracist pedagogy, so also is the painful engagement with personal experience, with microaggressions both committed and endured. Until we have unpacked and named the privileges we have taken for granted, the oppressions and slights we have borne, we are likely to unwittingly relive and respond to unnamed behaviors. This requires a far deeper level of discourse on race than the theoretical and academic. We should engage in a courageous exchange of personal and collective narratives that have the potential to reveal, through critical analysis, privilege, and assumptions of power.

Alladin (1996) observes inevitable conflict when race and power are placed on the table. He writes, "antiracist education is oppositional, therefore controversy is inevitable" (p. 160). If we have the courage to place the personal, and not just the theoretical, at the center of our discourse, then we should anticipate conflict and be prepared to understand its racialized roots. Conflict resolution is an essential component of antiracist pedagogy to maximize the positive, constructive potential of conflict, while guarding against conflict's negative and destructive effects. In building a democratic practice, it is only with the ability to explicitly address inequities based on race and power that its seeds of possibility will be nurtured and bear fruit.

References

Alladin, M. *Racism in Canadian Schools*. New York: Harcourt Brace, 1996.

Baptiste, I. "Exploring the Limits of Democratic Participation: Prudent and Decisive Use of Authority in Adult Education." In D. Ntiri (ed.), *Models for Adult and Lifelong Learning, Vol. 3—Politicization and Democratization of Adult Education* (pp. 1–34). Detroit: Office of Adult and Lifelong Learning Research, Wayne State University, 2001.

Baptiste, I., and Brookfield, S. "'Your So Called Democracy Is Hypocritical Because You Can Always Fail Us': Learning and Living Democratic Contradictions in Graduate Adult Education." In Proceedings of the 1997 International SCUTREA Conference. London: Standing Conference on University Teaching and Research in the Education of Adults, 1997.

Bronte de Avila, E., Caron, T., Flanagan, P., Frer, D., Heaney, T., Hyland, N., Kerstein, S., et al. "Democratizing Learning: Learning Participatory Graduate Education." In P. Campbell and B. Burnaby (eds.), *Participatory Practices in Adult Education* (pp. 221–236). Mahwah, N.J.: Lawrence Erlbaum, 2001.

Brookfield, S. *The Power of Critical Theory: Liberating Adult Learning and Teaching*. San Francisco: Jossey-Bass, 2005.

Colin, S.A.J., III, and Heaney, T. "Negotiating the Democratic Classroom." In C. Hansman and P. Sissel (eds.), *Understanding and Negotiating the Political Landscape of Adult Education*. New Directions for Adult and Continuing Education, no. 91 (pp. 29–38). San Francisco: Jossey-Bass, 2001.

Delgado, R. "Legal Storytelling: Storytelling for Oppositionists and Others: A Plea for Narrative." *Michigan Law Review*, 1989, 87, 2411–2459.

Delgado, R., and Stefancic, J. (eds.). *Critical Race Theory: The Cutting Edge*. Philadelphia: Temple University Press, 2000.

Dixson, A. D., and Rousseau, C. K. (eds.). *Critical Race Theory in Education*. New York: Routledge, 2006.

Freeman, A. D. "Legitimizing Racial Discrimination Through Antidiscrimination Law: A Critical Review of Supreme Court Doctrine." *Minnesota Law Review*, 1977–1978, 62, 1049–1120.

Grossman, R. "Obama in Awkward Spot in Dialogue on Prejudice." *Chicago Tribune*, October 5, 2009, Retrieved April 15, 2010 from http://www.chicagotribune.com/news/opinion/chi-oped1005temperamentoct05,0,6382664.story.

Lindeman, E. *The Meaning of Adult Education*. Norman: Oklahoma Research Center for Continuing Professional and Higher Education, 1961.

Nicholas, P., and Simon, R. "Obama Addresses Congress on Health Care: The Time for Games Has Passed." *Chicago Tribune*, Sept. 10, 2009, Retreived April 15, 2010 from http://www.chicagotribune.com/news/chi-tc-nw-obama-health-0909-0910 sep10,0,118416.story.

Solórzano, D., Ceja, M., and Yosso, T. "Critical Race Theory, Microaggressions, and Campus Racial Climate: The Experiences of African American College Students." *Journal of Negro Education*, 2000, 69(1/2), 60–73.

DIANNE RAMDEHOLL *is an assistant professor in educational studies at the Harry Van Arsdale Center for Labor Studies, Empire State College.*

TANIA GIORDANI *is professor of adult education at College of Lake County.*

THOMAS HEANEY *is an associate professor and director of the Adult Education Doctoral Program at National-Louis University.*

WENDY YANOW *is adjunct faculty and a consultant in adult education.*

7

*This research builds on a connection between adult educa-
tion and democracy by exploring best practices in shared
governance in a major venue of adult education—the
academy. Its purpose is to enhance democratic practices
within the university and encourage the creation of new
structures for shared decision making.*

Democracy, Shared Governance, and
the University

Thomas Heaney

Many colleges and universities across the country are dealing with fiscal
crises and other pressures by renewing their commitment to strategic planning and clarifying their institutional missions and visions. In times of
upheaval and change, attention is inevitably drawn to how decisions are
made and by whom. By focusing on those who have nurtured a democratic
practice in the academy, this chapter aims to assist stakeholders in the
nation's colleges and universities as they address the challenges of institutional governance.

Faculty governance has been a defining feature of most American colleges and universities for several generations. Faculties have organized independent deliberative bodies—a senate or an association, for example—outside
the previously existing administrative structures where decisions had been
and largely have continued to be made. Decisions, even in areas identified by
faculty as its own "primary jurisdiction," have been generally subject to subsequent approval by a dean, provost, or president, leaving faculty frequently
in conflict with administration. Shared governance was meant to change all
that by bringing faculty, administration, and other stakeholders to the same
planning table, but the addition of faculty to an already established governance structure relatively late in the history of the university, and almost as
an afterthought, was problematic from the start.

Although some bemoan the lethargic pace of decision making whenever faculty is involved, faculty has insisted that its involvement in decision
making is essential if academic freedom and educational quality are to be
maintained. The university is one of the world's oldest organizations and

NEW DIRECTIONS FOR ADULT AND CONTINUING EDUCATION, no. 128, Winter 2010 © 2010 Wiley Periodicals, Inc.
Published online in Wiley Online Library (wileyonlinelibrary.com) • DOI: 10.1002/ace.392

has withstood various external pressures, including those of a changing marketplace, by a deliberative and consensual decision-making approach.

In consultation with staff at the Higher Learning Commission, I identified four institutions seeking to involve all constituencies at the planning table as part of their participation in the Academic Quality Improvement Program (AQIP). Through observation, interviews, and focus groups with representative stakeholders, I examined the strengths and weaknesses of their various approaches to and understandings of shared governance. I asked, in each instance, how shared governance balanced maximum participation with timely efficiency.

This study was premised on an assumption that today's universities and community colleges are adult education institutions—learning organizations in which all stakeholders are engaged in the production and the critical assessment of knowledge. An emphasis on building democracy in early adult education literature (Brookfield, 1987; Cunningham, 1993; Heaney, 1992; Horton, 1973) provided a conceptual basis for understanding how these institutions of higher learning could only be strengthened by a commitment to democratic practices. Eduard Lindeman (1961) promoted the practice of adult education on the principle that participation in decision-making demands informed representation at the planning table. Education is critical to the development of reasoned and shared governance. The effectiveness of widespread participation in decision making, such as democracy requires, demands ongoing and timely strategies for adults to reflect on and learn from their experiences and the experiences of others. For Lindeman, what distinguished adult education from other learning activities is the fact that it is integral to the struggle for democracy and shared governance.

Looking for Best Practices in the Academy

I visited three universities and one community college, all in the Midwest. Each of these institutions was accredited by the Higher Learning Commission through the Academic Quality Improvement Program (AQIP) and had undertaken as an AQIP Action Project the involvement of all constituencies in decision making. In the following the names of these institutions and the people within them have been changed. In each institution I conducted a small, multistakeholder focus group and follow-up interviews. The following is provided to give a sense of the context within which full-time faculty and adjuncts, staff, administration, and students sought to create structures for shared decision making.

Lakeside College is a comprehensive community college, emphasizing programs that prepare students for transfer or career entry. One-third of its faculty—approximately 250—is full time and unionized. The college serves over 8,000 students. Lakeside has adhered to a philosophy of "shared decision making" since its inception in the 1980s, although the current structures for supporting this philosophy are fairly recent and evolving.

Southwell University, named after the Jesuit poet Robert Southwell, serves a diverse ethnic, racial, and religious community with a focus on liberal arts and professional education. It was founded in the late 1800s to provide a quality liberal arts education for men and women. With 150 full time faculty, the university currently serves over 5,000 students in undergraduate, graduate, and doctoral degree programs. Shared governance is new to Southwell, where governance was formerly the domain of a hierarchical religious order.

Hempleton is a five-campus university located in four states and founded on principles of liberal arts, experiential learning, and social justice. Student population varies at each campus, ranging from about 200 at the smallest to over 5,000 at the largest. Each campus has its own distinct academic programs, community life, and regional or national identity. The campus included in this study had about 3,000 students and 125 full time faculty.

Rockton University is a liberal arts university with over 5000 students and 110 full time faculty. Shared governance was a two-year AQIP Action Project that resulted in enhanced communications and dialogue among stakeholders, but in no structural changes. That project is now retired.

Unveiling the Complexity

Four broad themes emerged from this study:

- There were varied interpretations of "shared governance" and its effectiveness, both between and within institutions.
- There were common dispositions that are part of the core culture in institutions striving to involve all stakeholders.
- There was general agreement on several structural components of shared governance.
- Authority and responsibility continue to be a source of tension, even in well-functioning systems.

Finding Common Ground. There was a wide range of meanings ascribed to "shared governance." Rockton has a Faculty Assembly that is only advisory to the provost and president. Lakeside, on the other hand, has a constitutionally empowered configuration of units that include representation of all stakeholders that both advise and have specified executive authority.

Rockton University engaged in consultative decision making (Tierney and Minor, 2003). The emphasis here was on communication before decisions were made, but there was little doubt that most decisions would be made by administration. Unlike Rockton, the other three institutions in this study clearly aspired to fully collaborative decision making, although their understanding of collaboration differed significantly. Nancy, a faculty member at Southwell University, stated, "I'm not always sure the administration understands what shared governance means the same way we do. We understand that there are some decisions that are the responsibility of administrators, but we also believe that some decisions ultimately belong to faculty. I'm not sure you (speaking to the provost) always agree with this."

The provost responded that most academic decisions were "primarily faculty-driven," but added that financial and legal considerations brought administrators "into play." The fact that faculty and administration, by reason of their positions, focus on different concerns and interests can skew their assessment of how well shared governance is working. Minor (2005), in a study of 103 colleges and universities, found that more than 75% of provosts thought shared governance was working, while 75% of faculty did not. This was confirmed at Lakeside College by Robert, a member of the faculty, who said, "Inevitably, administrators think shared governance is working better than faculty or staff." Joyce, a leader of the faculty union at the same college, provided a rationale for this when she said, "It's not surprising that the group ultimately making the decision will believe that shared governance is working."

Common Dispositions. Before looking at structural issues, participants in this study gave great emphasis to dispositions, common understandings, and relationships that were essential to bringing groups with such varied interests and skills to the planning table. Foremost among these was the ability to transcend the provincialism of self-interest, as well as the ability to create procedural justice and a culture of trust.

Balancing Institutional and Constituent Interests. In each institution, faculty, staff, and students elected representatives to governance, whereas administrators were ex officio. Each stakeholder at the planning table was expected to represent the interests of constituents, but at the same time needed to represent the best interests of the institution as a whole. This tension requires balance; balance is new to faculty who, until now, only had to consider their own interests. As Joyce said, "If administration consulted the faculty, they expected the faculty to speak for faculty. That's it." Now, under shared governance, faculty are still expected to express faculty interests and concerns, but also engage in discourse that weaves those interests into the larger tapestry of the overall interests of the college or university.

Other factors can complicate this balance. Lakeside College has a faculty union, the role of which has changed in significant ways under shared governance. As a union, the focus is almost exclusively on compensation and workload issues. Now the union is represented on the College Council where, as Joyce indicated, "we're involved in the broader picture."

Procedural Justice and the Maintenance of Trust. Birnbaum (2004) uses the term "procedural justice" to refer to the perceived fairness of processes through which organizational decisions are made. He notes that "fairness of procedure has no objective criteria—it is what the members of the group believe it to be" (p. 13). Nancy, a faculty member at Southwell, talked about a vocal minority who saw shared decision making as taking power from faculty. She said, "(faculty) thought we'd been co-opted. The fact is, we never had power to begin with and now we have tremendous influence." What is described here is nothing less than a cultural shift. The underlying disposition in achieving these changes is trust.

"Trust is an element in a consensual relationship in which there is equal risk and equal benefit as perceived by the parties involved, and there is a belief that the other party will act in a reciprocal manner" (Pope, 2004, p. 76). Trust emerges over time and requires constant vigilance to be maintained. At Southwell University there was, in the beginning, a great deal of skepticism among faculty who believed that administration had no real interest in opening up the hundred-year-old, hierarchical decision-making apparatus. Nancy said, "I'd describe where we are now as 'cautious trust.'" Cautious is also the operative word when Joyce said, "We didn't go into this blind. We were willing to take a chance, but we were vigilant." This did not mean that faculty always got what they wanted; it meant that free and open debate had occurred and that any rejection by administration of a faculty or staff position was always accompanied by a rationale that faculty could understand.

Agreements on Structure. The structures and procedures of shared governance were varied, with each institution deriving organizational patterns from their own mission and values. Which decisions are entrusted to a committee and which stakeholders sit on that committee varied greatly, but there were, nonetheless, structural characteristics each institution held in common.

Loosely Coupled System. Tierney (2001) argued that the point in shared governance is not to create a more tightly coupled system, but to improve decision making within a loosely coupled system. He elaborates on this in an article written with Minor:

> Colleges and universities exist in loosely coupled environments. A mistaken tendency among those attempting to improve faculty governance is to try to tighten this loose coupling . . . Effective governance is defined not so much by the presence of an efficient structure or by the number of votes the faculty concludes in a year. Effective governance pertains more to the understanding and management of meaning such that the core values of the faculty and of the institution are not merely preserved, but advanced (Tierney and Minor, 2004, p. 92).

All the institutions in this study moved slowly in the creation of structures for shared governance. They avoided highly centralized units that would preempt the multiple units of governance already in place. They recognized the need to balance clarity of structure with the flexibility needed to engage all stakeholders in the work of governance.

Maintaining communications within and between all constituencies is more important than rigid structural definitions. These communications and frequent involvement of all segments of the community are what Tierney has described as "loose coupling." Nancy, who is the chair of the Faculty Caucus and a representative to the University Senate at Southwell, spoke about her role in "coupling" the various systems in which she is involved: "The most important task I've taken on is to keep the faculty in the loop. It doesn't make any difference when (faculty) representatives are fully engaged at the table, if the faculty as a whole don't perceive the process as inclusive."

Retaining Separate Interest Groups. Faculty at each institution sought clarity about what decisions pertain to the entire community, and what decisions are best left to faculty (Engstrand, 2005). Davis and Page (2006), reflecting on the American Association of University Professors' (AAUP) *Red Book* and other accreditation documents, conclude that any new governance structure would have to enable the faculty (1) to make its own regulations governing matters within its jurisdiction (*faculty governance*), and (2) to participate in decision making with other constituencies involving broader issues within the institution (*shared governance*). The aim is to allow each constituency to identify and articulate its interests/concerns and provide a forum for the integration of these interests with the interests of the larger university or college community.

Joyce reflects this aim in her comment about the faculty union's concerns at Lakeside, "There was apprehension in 2002 that the College Council would undercut the union and the Faculty Association. In fact, the Council gave renewed life to both organizations. They are the voice of faculty, the place where common interests are identified."

The maintenance of strong and organized caucuses representing various constituencies was found to be an essential communications link, bringing each stakeholder's voice to the planning table.

Becoming a Learning Organization. Participants in shared governance require access to information before they can effectively make decisions. Senates and councils become sites of learning and adult education as members struggle to understand the complexity of budgets, facilities management, human resources, along with academic standards and curricula. Representatives at the planning table committed themselves to providing information and being informed by others.

In addition to ongoing and substantial learning related to planning and decision making, there was also a need to learn how to govern democratically. Southwell was the only institution in this study, however, that had provided formal training in governance, initially for members of the University Senate, and later for anyone in the university community on a voluntary basis. Referring to the fact that Southwell had been ruled by a hierarchical religious order for almost 100 years, Gene, the provost, said, "Training was very important for all of us, especially given our history."

New Directions for Adult and Continuing Education • DOI: 10.1002/ace

Training at Southwell was organized by the business faculty, building largely on the work of Fisher, Ury, and Patton (1991) and the Interest-Based Strategy widely used in business and labor organizations. Of the latter Nancy said, "The most valuable training sessions for me were the workshops we had on "Interest-Based Strategy." It has taken a while for it to become part of our culture, but it has changed the way we think about issues, especially when we find ourselves in disagreement with Gene" (the provost).

Although other institutions did not provide formal training, participants in the study expressed a reliance on the expertise of colleagues for whom the knowledge of group dynamics, democratic social change, or learning organizations was central to their disciplines. Joyce pointed to the contribution she and other members of the union had made at Lakeside based on their experiences with negotiations. Shared governance nurtured acknowledgment of and respect for the experiences of faculty, staff, and administration, so that while structured training did not occur, informal and experiential learning was broadly acknowledged as a by-product of their collaborative structures of governance.

Tension between the Need to Respond Quickly and Deliberative Involvement. The tendency in a loosely coupled system can be to multiply units of governance, layering shared governance units on top of single stakeholder units until the burgeoning structure grinds to a halt. This is the challenge posed by complexity: on the one hand, full participation by all stakeholders is demanded by shared governance; on the other hand, deliberate speed and agility remain desirable institutional characteristics.

Closing the circle, taking the time needed to communicate with constituents, seems at times to compromise agility. However, most participants in shared governance believed that, as regular patterns of communication were developed, it became easier to balance agility with full deliberation. Balance was the key: not valuing agility or full deliberation to the exclusion of the other. As Birnbaum (2004) notes, "The greatest danger to higher education may not be that decisions are made too slowly because of the drag of consultation, but that they are made too swiftly and without regard for institutional core values" (p. 7).

Authority and Responsibility. People who are accountable for decisions must have the authority to make them. However, those with authority to make decisions can make them in an environment that solicits the involvement of all stakeholders. Participants understood that power and authority remain factors in shared governance.

Power Issues Remain. Joyce, a faculty union representative at Lakeside, said, "There are more people involved in making decisions now, but we're not so naive as to think that we've leveled the playing field. A few still hold the power to make the final decisions." Margaret confirmed this when she said, "My authority as president has not diminished. The board still holds me accountable, but I make better decisions after getting the input from the college community." Tom, speaking from a faculty point of view, confirmed both Joyce and Margaret in saying, "We don't think we're all equal when we meet. There might be ten faculty members on the Senate, but only one president. We know that the president is the one who will be held accountable for most of our decisions. But we also know that the president cannot lead the university without the faculty behind him."

Multistakeholder units of governance found it important to identify up front who was ultimately held accountable for each decision made. As Robert indicated, "When we go through the agenda, we begin by asking ourselves, 'Whose decision is this?'" At Southwell, their interest-based strategy began with identifying and valuing everyone's interests, then analyzing what decisions can maximally respect those interests. Although the process in many instances is consultative, nonetheless the person with authority to make the decision is usually able to exercise that responsibility to the satisfaction of all or most of those at the table.

Power remains an issue, certainly at Rockton where as the provost said, "the faculty do vote, but they're all recommendations. So in essence the votes are non-binding." It also remains an issue for stakeholders with the least power. As Todd indicated, "I can't say that students really feel empowered by all of this. We're just better informed."

Decision Making versus Advisory Roles. The presence of power can lead to frustrations. Robert, a faculty member at Lakeside, pointed out, "We came to learn that for faculty to commit to the process, we needed to have executive authority as well. We needed to be able to do something, take action, make something happen." Speaking of the importance of executive authority to faculty, Duderstadt (2004) wrote, "Advisory bodies, paid only lip service by the administration or board of trustees, will rarely attract the attention or engage the participation of those faculty most actively engaged in scholarship and teaching. Hence a key to effective governance is to provide faculty bodies with executive rather than merely advisory authority, thereby attracting the active participation of the university's leading faculty members" (p. 84).

Administration and Faculty Power. Few decisions are the prerogative of only one constituency. As Richard, a faculty member at Lakeside, noted, "There were some areas we felt were the faculty's domain, especially curriculum, academic policy. What we've learned from our new governance structures is that these academic matters also have financial implications. They impact support systems in the college. We need to consult with administrators and staff, even in developing curriculum. With these folks at the table, we not only save time, but we make better decisions."

For many initially this was counterintuitive. Some thought that inviting administrators and staff to sit at the planning table would co-opt faculty, undermine faculty's jurisdiction over the curriculum. However, when faculty makes plans alone, only its own interests are on the table. The interests of other stakeholders do not surface until those plans are put forward to administration. Then there is "push-back," time wasted, and sometimes hostility. However, as Rodney noted, "With all the players in the room, there aren't any surprises." As Glotzbach (2001) wrote, "Sometimes faculty members believe that they increase their autonomy and authority by excluding administrators from deliberations until they have arrived at a position or crafted a proposal that has been endorsed by a faculty group. This tactic is, however, misguided and, in fact, achieves just the opposite of its intended effect. The power of administrators to say no is far greater when they are presented with a proposal or a recommendation they have had no part in developing" (Section 4, paragraph 3).

Discussion and Conclusions

Shared governance does not compromise administrators' or board members' rightful authority, neither does it lessen the faculty's "primary responsibility" for the overall curriculum, "the subject matter and methods of instruction," research, requirements for the degrees offered, faculty appointments, promotion and tenure, and "those aspects of student life which relate to the educational process" (American Association of University Professors, 2001, pp. 218–223). Shared governance honors these varied responsibilities and acknowledges the complex interweaving roles of faculty, administration, staff, and students in fulfilling the mission of the university.

Formal structures, councils, or senates do not of themselves give voice to faculty, staff, or students. It is the commitment of boards and administrators to listen to these stakeholders. "When values are not aligned, then the board may assert its prerogatives regardless of faculty sentiment, ignoring the structures that give voice to faculty sentiments" (Kaplan, 2004, p. 32). To achieve this alignment the academic community must become a learning organization informed by principles of adult education and commitment to ongoing development.

The dispositions of balancing institutional and constituent interests, procedural justice, and trust are what allowed structures of shared governance to work effectively. Effective structures were loosely coupled systems, which included some governing units with multiple stakeholders relevant to the task working together, and others that were separate interest units representing a single stakeholder.

Shared decision making required a more complex view of governance. Unlike the binary "we/they" of other models of governance, creating a common planning table with all relevant stakeholders demands a clear understanding of and respect for the various roles and responsibilities of each constituency. The planning table becomes an adult education classroom in which the roles of teacher and learner constantly shift.

New Directions for Adult and Continuing Education • DOI: 10.1002/ace

In its expanded role, faculty was called to statesmanship, rather than giving way to provincialism. It is faculty provincialism and administrative imperialism that are frequently identified as the major hurdles in creating shared governance (Baldridge, 1982). Even in the best of worlds faculty had to remain vigilant, guarding against administrative attempts to centralize power, especially when faced with a crisis. Decisions are more likely to be accepted when they do not challenge the interests and status of any stakeholder and are less likely to be accepted if they do (Birnbaum, 2004).

Navigating the tumultuous waters of university governance requires skill. Elected representatives in shared governance bodies at each of the participating institutions were chosen carefully on the basis of their ability and experience. Governing is difficult work and governing wisely is an acquired skill requiring a commitment to learning and reflective practice. Shared governance remains an ongoing task—one that depends on finding structures and procedures that sustain and deepen relationships of trust and understanding. There is widespread understanding that structure is less important than the underlying culture it supports. Although formal constitutions define structures, these documents cannot guarantee civility, trustworthiness, or transparency. With a commitment to these qualities of relationship and the effort to maintain them, the university can achieve its potential as an adult education institution, which engages students, faculty, and staff in creating the future democratically.

References

American Association of University Professors. *Policy Documents and Reports*. 9th ed. Washington, D.C.: American Association of University Professors, 2001.

Baldridge, J. V. "Shared Governance: A Fable about the Lost Magic Kingdom." *Academe*, 1982, 68(1), 12–15.

Birnbaum, R. "The End of Shared Governance: Looking Ahead or Looking Back." In W. G. Tierney and V. M. Lechuga (eds.), *Restructuring Shared Governance in Higher Education*. New Directions for Higher Education, no. 127, pp. 5–22. San Francisco: Jossey-Bass, 2004.

Brookfield, S. *Learning Democracy: Eduard Lindeman on Adult Education and Social Change*. Beckenham, Kent U.K.: Croom Helm, 1987.

Cunningham, P. M. "Let's Get Real: A Critical Look at the Practice of Adult Education." *Journal of Adult Education*, 1993, 22(1), 3–15.

Davis, L. K., and Page, D. L. "Governance Review Without Tears." Academe Online, 2006, 92(6). Retrieved March 23, 2010, from http://www.aaup.org/AAUP/pubsres/academe/2006/ND/Feat/Davi.htm

Duderstadt, J. J. "Governing the Twenty-First-Century University: A View from the Bridge." In W. G. Tierney (ed.), *Competing Conceptions of Academic Governance: Negotiating the Perfect Storm*. Baltimore: The Johns Hopkins University Press, 2004.

Engstrand, G. "A University Senate for All." Academe Online, 2005, 91(3). Retrieved March 23, 2010, from http://www.aaup.org/AAUP/pubsres/academe/2005/MJ/Feat/engs.htm

Fisher, R., Ury, W., and Patton, B. *Getting to Yes: Negotiating Agreement without Giving In*. 2nd ed. New York: Houghton Mifflin Company, 1991.

Glotzbach, P. A. "Conditions of Collaboration: A Dean's List of Dos and Don'ts." Academe Online, 2001, 87(3). Retrieved March 23, 2010, from http://www.aaup.org/AAUP/pubsres/academe/2001/MJ/Feat/Glot.htm

Heaney, T. "When Adult Education Stood for Democracy." *Adult Education Quarterly*, 1992, 43(1), 51–59.

Horton, M. "Decision-Making Processes." In N. Shimahara (ed.), *Educational Reconstructionism*. Columbus, Ohio: Merrill, 1973.

Kaplan, G.E. "Do Governance Structures Matter?" In W. G. Tierney and V. M. Lechuga (eds.), *Restructuring Shared Governance in Higher Education*. New Directions for Higher Education, no. 127, pp. 23–34. San Francisco: Jossey-Bass, 2004.

Lindeman, E. *The Meaning of Adult Education*. Norman: Oklahoma Research Center for Continuing Professional and Higher Education, 1961.

Minor, J. T. "Faculty Governance at Historically Black Colleges and Universities." Academe Online, 2005, 91(3). Retrieved March 23, 2010, from http://www.aaup.org/AAUP/pubsres/academe/2005/MJ/Feat/mino.htm

Pope, M. L. "A Conceptual Framework of Faculty Trust and Participation in Governance." In W. G. Tierney and V. M. Lechuga (eds.), *Restructuring Shared Governance in Higher Education*. New Directions for Higher Education, no. 127, pp. 75–84. San Francisco: Jossey-Bass, 2004.

Tierney, W. G. "Why Committees Don't Work: Creating a Structure for Change." Academe Online, 2001, 87(3). Retrieved March 23, 2010, from http://www.aaup.org/AAUP/pubsres/academe/2001/MJ/Feat/tier.html

Tierney, W. G., and Minor, J. T. "Challenges for Governance: A National Report." Los Angeles: Center for Higher Education Policy Analysis, 2003. Retrieved March 23, 2010, from http://www.usc.edu/dept/cheps

Tierney, W. G., and Minor, J. T. "A Cultural Perspective on Communications and Governance." In W. G. Tierney and V. M. Lechuga (eds.), *Restructuring Shared Governance in Higher Education*. New Directions for Higher Education, no. 127, pp. 85–94. San Francisco: Jossey-Bass, 2004.

THOMAS HEANEY *is an associate professor and director of the Adult Education Doctoral Program at National-Louis University in Chicago.*

The authors in this chapter promote the democratic principle of participatory decision making by asking who benefits and who should benefit from adult education program planning.

Democracy and Program Planning

Arthur L. Wilson, Ronald M. Cervero

Program planning is often described, but rarely experienced, as a routine set of activities intended to bring order and efficiency to the tasks of developing and organizing curricula and programs in adult, continuing, and workplace education. There are literally hundreds of articles and books over the last 75 years in the North American adult education literature that provide myriad methods, techniques, and strategies for planning and organizing various forms of adult education. In our reviews of these many models and theories of program planning (Cervero and Wilson, 1994, 2006; Wilson and Cervero, 1997), we have shown that despite the great variety of prescriptive details, most efforts actually represent a consistent underlying rational problem-solving logic prescribing specific but generic planning activities. The "formula," so to speak, is to define needs, use needs to set objectives, use objectives to select content, select teaching strategies to meet the objectives and deliver the content, and evaluate the results. No greater authority in curriculum theory than Ralph Tyler (1949) codified this scientifically rational planning logic in his concise statement of planning questions in 1949, although the systematic thinking of curriculum planning arose much earlier in the twentieth century. Tyler's four curriculum questions are still in print and use today because they provide effective principles for planning and organizing curricula and programs—at least partially so.

We would make two observations on the current state of planning theory in North American adult education. First, the prevailing logic of addressing planning tasks in the specified sequence—that is, to define needs to define objectives, use objectives to select content, evaluate the success in meeting the objectives—has had its most severe challenge by those questioning the requirement to address the planning steps in the prescribed

New Directions for Adult and Continuing Education, no. 128, Winter 2010 © 2010 Wiley Periodicals, Inc.
Published online in Wiley Online Library (wileyonlinelibrary.com) • DOI: 10.1002/ace.393

order. Cyril Houle still has the foremost and most eloquent position of understanding planning "as a complex of interacting elements, not a logical sequence of steps" (1972, p. 46). In general curriculum theory, this understanding of planning as decision making, as opposed to instrumental problem solving, is known as the deliberative movement. Even though the field of adult education committed intellectually to the Tylerian logic of sequenced steps (e.g., Knowles, 1950), whether the activities must be conducted in order or represent sets of "interacting elements" remains an active issue (e.g., Caffarella, 2002). Whereas both positions have merit for providing insights and directives for practice, empirically neither represents a fully adequate account of actual planning practice (Cervero and Wilson, 1994). We turn shortly to our understanding of planning.

But first, the debate just sketched is but a backdrop to our second observation: many adult education planning theorists have long espoused a democratic ethos as central to planning thinking and activity. Sometimes that democratic impulse has been implicit as in such prescriptions "to involve the learners." More often there are specific explanations or directives regarding a democratic process to planning such as Houle's (1972, p. 35) depiction of planning as "cooperative" or Knowles's (1970, p. 60) directive to base learning objectives on the "real needs and interests . . . as determined by a group that is representative of all participants . . . that there will be a maximum participation by all members in sharing responsibility for making and carrying out decisions." Indeed, when we examined the evolution of specific planning activities (e.g., assessing needs, establishing objectives, developing curriculum, administering programs, and evaluating results), each activity had its own history and specifications as to what "democratic" meant (Cervero and Wilson, 2006). The democratic ethos is clearly evident in North American planning theory. Nevertheless, it is just as evident that such ethos often resides as implied assumptions, sometimes stated beliefs, and often mostly as hoped for effects and consequences.

We have developed an understanding of planning practice that takes advantage of the insights of the Tylerian and deliberative positions but moves on to wrangle with the often unsaid but very influential questions of power and interests in planning practice (Cervero and Wilson, 1994, 2006). We have consistently espoused the general democratic ethos of the field while also trying to understand what that looks like in actual practice. To that end we have promoted a democratic principle of participatory decision making by asking who benefits and who should benefit from our work as adult educators. We will briefly review our understanding of adult education program planning to focus on the democratic ethos we promote. Because each of us has served as department chairs, and one as an associate dean, in higher education, we will then examine some of our experiences in promoting shared decision making.

New Directions for Adult and Continuing Education • DOI: 10.1002/ace

Working the Planning Table in Theory

We have already provided some sense of how we think about planning and how we developed our understanding. Here we outline some of our major tenets to present the democratic ethical principles we hope to embody in our work as theorists and practitioners in adult education.

We have developed the image of "working the planning table" (Cervero and Wilson, 1998, 2006) to capture the social, political, ethical, and organizational dimensions of planning practice: that is, to put real people at real planning tables, planning in real organizational settings. Too often planning has been presented academically as a disembodied set of tasks that some generic planner conducts, or at best, a consensually agreeable group of people rationally deciding what to plan. Our own experience as well as that of our colleagues and students has shown us that the traditional instrumental and deliberative accounts of practice were helpful but limited in understanding what adult education planning was really like. Because every setting and educational activity often represents unique interplays of organizational mandates, people's interests, and relations of power, we have described program planning in adult education as a social process of negotiating interests within relations of power in organizational settings of various kinds (Cervero and Wilson, 1994, 2006). Four concepts structure our understanding of planning practice: power, interests, negotiation, and ethical commitment to democratic principles. Because we believe that theory should both account for what actually happens in practice as well as provide a guide to action (Foley, 1999), we have used these concepts to understand what real planners do in actual planning as well as recommend what they should be doing to nurture substantively democratic planning.

We describe planners as working planning tables because it is at the literal and metaphorical planning tables that planners make judgments with other people about educational program purposes, contents, audiences, and formats in socially and organizationally structured relationships of power. Putting planners and other people at planning tables helps to show that power relations shape how decisions are made about educational programs, who gets to make such decisions, and why they turn out the way they do. Everyone involved in educational planning represents two sociopolitical dimensions of activity: a capacity to act (power) because of their position and participation in relatively enduring social and organizational relationships and specific sets of concerns and motivations (interests) that planners and others bring to the table about what should be done. Planners' primary activity in planning is negotiating whereby they come to agreement, whether consensual, conflictual, or some combination thereof, about what to do depending upon who represents which interests and who has what power to act. Planners working planning tables produce two outcomes: Planners negotiate with specific interests to determine the specific features of educational programs as well as negotiate the power relations themselves, seeking to maintain or alter the sociopolitical organizational working relationships of the planners.

Because of the importance of negotiating power relations and interests in influencing decisions, it really matters who gets to the planning table. We have argued (Cervero and Wilson, 1994, 2001, 2006) that people's interests are causally related to the practical judgments planners make about what to do and the specific features of planned programs. Consequently, to embody a democratic adult education ethos, we believe that politically astute planning in adult education anticipates the role of power in planning and requires a steadfast commitment to substantive democratic participation in decision making. Substantive democratic participation means making an ethical commitment about who should be at the table and who should benefit from the educational program. That has been our stance since we first began theorizing planning as a political practice (Cervero and Wilson, 1994). We have developed specific tactics for planners to interrogate their practice in terms of democratic decision making: Are all potential and relevant interests represented at the planning table, are the representatives the best available, and who should be at the planning table but is not? In theory, such tactics should enhance democratic planning. In practice we have had little opportunity to investigate the worthiness and practicality of such tactical recommendations in fostering more democratic participation in educational program planning except through the reflection on our own practice, which we will turn to next. We are aware, however, that no one democratic principle can be expected to encompass all situations (Sork, 1996) that the traditional adult education democratic principle of participation has been expected to do. But we believe we have a malleable concept that allows for expansion and contraction depending on the situation. As others, we believe that in nearly every situation there is usually some opportunity, no matter how small, to enact democratic principles of participation (Youngman, 1996).

Working Planning Tables in Practice

In addition to our professorial scholarly, teaching, and extension activities, each of us has spent a significant amount of the past ten years in academic leadership positions. Ron was head of the Department of Adult Education and then the reorganized Department of Lifelong Education, Administration, and Policy for seven and a half years at the University of Georgia. He is now associate dean for outreach and engagement in the College of Education. From 2000–2007 Arthur was program leader for Adult and Extension Education in the Department of Education in the College of Agriculture and Life Sciences at Cornell University before becoming department chair. Although both of us have had other leadership experiences, we focus here on our academic leadership roles. In fact, it is a bit ironic that we wrote our last book during this past decade. Given our responsibilities, there have been many times when one of us would call the other to say, "Damn, I wish we weren't so right about this power and interest stuff!" We have lived a lot of what we say and here we share some of that. Our focus will be on our successes or lack thereof in promoting and embodying substantive democratic participation.

We examine experiences we have had in one of the more contentious areas of higher education administration: awarding of pay raises on meritocratic principles. The adage that "no where do so many fight so viciously for so little" does really often characterize salary competition in higher education. Some might not consider salary improvement decisions an example of program planning. But educational leaders who are committed to participatory decision making have to help develop a culture in which such decisions are more of a norm rather than an exception. In this sense we are examining program planning in larger organizational terms, not just the discrete development and delivery of a contained curriculum, as is often the focus of Tylerian, deliberative, and critical models of planning. Thus, our focus is the overall development of a culture of shared and participatory decision making through a very specific set of practices around a specific set of administrative responsibilities.

Every department head or chair has had to make decisions about salary improvements that Ron had to in his tenure as a department head. In many universities allegedly meritocratic salary decisions are contentious, secretive, autocratic, and, yes, unfair and even vengeful at times. Collegial relations can be disrupted, even destroyed, and departmental functioning can become impaired in feuds over salary. The adage quoted above can really play out in very destabilizing ways. Ron was very aware of the contentious nature of salary decisions and, wanting to embody shared decision making in departmental practices, negotiated with departmental faculty a set of principles and processes by which salary improvement decisions were made in consultation with faculty rather than "behind their backs," so to speak. To that end, the department developed a set of principles to guide the activity; defined materials required in the assessment; defined criteria for evaluating research, teaching, and service; and developed algorithms for allocating actual dollar amounts based on individual faculty activities and the available pool of dollars assigned to the department for raises. The procedures developed for accomplishing shared decision making are extensive and beyond the scope of our intentions for this effort. The principles guiding the process, however, will provide an indication of how Ron embodied a shared decision-making ethos in determining appropriate raises for individual faculty.

There were specific criteria for evaluating faculty activity in research, teaching, and service: does not meet expectations, meets expectations, exceeds expectations, exceptional. In assessing the documentation for each of the major categories of professorial activity, Ron sought to promote "faculty development" in terms of providing an opportunity for an annual discussion for faculty members' past activities and future goals and needs. This discussion also provided "capacity building" by examining the individuals' activities in terms of the department's needs and goals. The two principles explicitly representing the shared decision-making ethos were those of "transparency" and "accountability." In terms of transparency the annual review process was clearly delineated in terms of who was involved and how the process was conducted. In terms of accountability, Ron had to justify his assessment of each faculty member to a committee of program coordinators, which helped to protect individual faculty members from any intentional or unintentional bias from Ron.

In terms of embodying our ethical stance, Ron was trying to include all the interests of relevant parties in the decision making: each individual faculty member, Ron as head of the department, and program area coordinators of each individual faculty member. All had pertinent interests in the decision making and each was at some portion of the planning table where decisions were being made. They clearly are the best representatives available and stand to benefit the most from the decision making. It could be argued, however, that other interested parties, who might be affected by the decision making, were not at the planning table. For example, it seems self-evident that the department's students stand to benefit, or not, from the effect of salary decision making on subsequent faculty performance. Were students at the table? There can be considerable argument regarding such a role for students. For our purposes we would say, although not actually present at the decision tables, they were, however, represented by those who were in the sense that all three interested parties would have students as their professional concerns. Similar observations might be made about the staff of the department or the organizations that might ultimately employ graduates of the program or the communities in which graduates might live someday, and so on. Where such representation might be viewed as a dodge, it does conform to our notion of "best available representative." We do note, however, as an ethical and practical concern, that there is a limit to the principle of including all possible stakeholders in that, as Stanley Fish notes (2007), including all possible stakeholders is utopian in practice because to try to do so actually leads to "paralysis."

Arthur has two related experiences. First, as an assistant professor at another university, he participated in a salary improvement system that was similar to the one Ron helped to devise at Georgia. Acceptable faculty activities, as defined by the department faculty, in research, teaching, and service were arrayed and ranked by point value in order of importance. For example, in terms of research, refereed journal articles had higher point values than a conference presentation; published books earned more points than journal articles. Teaching and service were likewise arrayed. Each department's salary improvement pool was allocated based on the sum of all of the faculty's salaries, which was then to be awarded meritocratically according to point totals of individual faculty activity for the previous year. There were a number of powerful faculty in this department, however, including one current and two ex-deans. These deans and other long-tenured faculty argued that because their higher salaries actually *increased* the pool available for merit distribution they therefore deserved *automatically* the actual dollar amount that their higher salaries contributed to the salary pool *before* any remaining dollars were distributed for merit. For example, if the merit pool were 3% of the sum of all the salaries in the department, each professor would contribute differentially according to their actual salary. Faculty A, making $100,000 a year would "contribute" $3,000 to the merit pool whereas Faculty B making $30,000 a year would contribute $900 dollars to the pool. Before merit was determined according to the point system, Faculty A would automatically receive a $3,000 raise whereas Faculty B would only gain $900. Thus, the higher-paid faculty "convinced"—that is, in our analysis, they used their power to further financial interests—the department to approve a corollary to the merit process that mandated that each faculty automatically got back that portion of the raise pool that their actual salary contributed to it before any allocations were made for merit. By definition, higher-salaried faculty automatically got a larger portion of the raise pool. Because their larger salary contributed more dollars to the pool, higher-salaried faculty always got more actual dollars as raises. This maneuver not only defeated the original purpose of the point system to award raises solely for achievement, it also effectively maintained discrepancies in salary. This example shows how a putatively rational system designed to promote equality of opportunity actually can be distorted by those with more power to meet their interests, in this case to increase higher salaries at a greater rate. Under the guise of consensus decision making, there was no shared decision making or representation of anyone's interests other than that of the higher-salaried faculty who had more power than other faculty.

When Arthur became chair at Cornell he took on the same merit raise responsibilities Ron had at Georgia. The Department of Education at Cornell had formed decades earlier as a collection of various program areas such as educational foundations, educational psychology, curriculum and instruction, teacher education, agricultural education, and adult and extension education. With a large faculty and many programs, competition for resources was normal. Traditionally, salary improvement decision making has largely been a cloaked process, controlled by the department chair. After announcements were made at the university level about the percentage increase available for merit increases, faculty would receive two to three months later a confidential letter communicating their salary increase. Typically faculty did not discuss among themselves or with the chair how the decisions got made. This is the tradition Arthur inherited when he became chair. He has done very little to change it. He and the department adminis-trator examined the annual reports of each faculty member. They then ranked them according to a scale of "very productive," "productive," "under productive," based on examining each faculty's scholarly production, teach-ing evaluations, and service records. When possible, which meant gaining the deans' approval, adjustments were made for past gender and race inequities, of which there were several. But there was no shared decision making except upward with the deans, and no accountability or trans-parency at the department level. Arthur still contends that the decisions were appropriate and that those who met and exceeded the activity criteria got the most meritocratic raises. Nevertheless, he readily agrees the salary decisions were neither transparent nor accountable. In this situation, Arthur and the administrative manager were representing all the interests of affected parties as well as all the others who stood to benefit or not from their activities such as the college and university administrations as well as past, present, and future students. That is a very questionable proposition, but one that often characterizes such decision making in higher education. The decisions made in this case were still likely the best ones in terms of allocating a meritocratic system and correcting for structural distortions as a result of gender and race because Arthur maintains that the differing power and interests of individual faculty would have produced distortions in the allocations, as it had in the previous example. But the unilateral deci-sion making clearly violates principles of shared decision making, trans-parency, and accountability. Being fair, rational, and transparent about money just does not occur easily.

Closing Note

Fish (2007) questions the inclusion of stakeholders in university decision making, arguing that good university functioning is not typically a function of shared governance, indeed, often quite the opposite. Ron's experience at Georgia provides evidence that even in something as secretive and compet-itive as salary improvement, shared decision making, transparency, and accountability can be enacted. Arthur's experience of "carrying on the Cornell tradition" clearly violates any notion of participatory decision making even though it was efficient and, by his account, effective in fairly distributing salary raises. Therefore, we end with ethical conundrums. In one case, the participatory principle provided a rational system and appropriate guidance to manage shared governance. In a similar system those with the most power distorted, undermined, and exploited an alleged system of equitable decision making. And finally, a third example showed how power was used to further equity interests but was neither transparent nor accountable. Because people make decisions about what to do, rational planning is subject to the distortions of power and interests. Moreover, because of *that*, we still argue that the democratic principle of involving all whom we can in making decisions is the ethical stance that should guide planning despite the supporting and counterfactual experiences described in this chapter.

References

Caffarella, R. *Planning Programs for Adult Learners: A Practical Guide for Educators, Trainers, and Staff Developers.* San Francisco: Jossey-Bass, 2002.

Cervero, R., and Wilson, A. *Planning Responsibly for Adult Education: A Guide to Negotiating Power and Interests.* San Francisco: Jossey-Bass, 1994.

Cervero, R., and Wilson, A. "Working the Planning Table: The Political Practice of Adult Education." *Studies in Continuing Education,* 1998, 20(1), 5–21.

Cervero, R., and Wilson, A. (eds.) *Power in Practice: Adult Education and the Struggle for Knowledge and Power in Society.* San Francisco: Jossey-Bass, 2001.

Cervero, R., and Wilson, A. *Working the Planning Table: Negotiating Democratically for Adult, Continuing and Workplace Education.* San Francisco: Jossey-Bass, 2006.

Fish, S. "Shared Governance: Democracy is Not an Educational Idea." *Change: The Magazine of Higher Education,* March–April, 2007. Retrieved June 9, 2007, from http://www.changemag.org/Archives/Back%20Issues/March-April%202007/full-shared-governance.html

Foley, G. *Strategic Learning: Understanding and Facilitating Organizational Change.* Sydney: Centre for Popular Education, 1999.

Houle, C. *The Design of Education.* San Francisco: Jossey-Bass, 1972.

Knowles, M. *Informal Adult Education.* New York: AAAE, 1950.

Knowles, M. *The Modern Practice of Adult Education: Andragogy Versus Pedagogy.* New York: Association Press, 1970.

Sork, T. "Negotiating Power and Interests in Planning: A Critical Perspective." In R. Cervero and A. Wilson (eds.), *What Really Matters in Adult Education Program Planning: Lessons in Negotiating Power and Interests,* pp. 81–90. San Francisco: Jossey-Bass, 1996.

Tyler, R. *Basic Principles of Curriculum and Instruction.* Chicago: University of Chicago Press, 1949.

Wilson, A., and Cervero, R. "The Song Remains the Same: The Selective Tradition of Technical Rationality in Adult Education Program Planning." *International Journal of Lifelong Education,* 1997, 16(2), 84–108.

Youngman, F. "A Transformative Political Economy of Adult Education." In P. Wangoola and F. Youngman (eds.), *Towards a Transformative Political Economy of Adult Education: Theoretical and Practical Challenges,* pp. 3–30. DeKalb: Northern Illinois University, LEPS Press, 1996.

ARTHUR L. WILSON *is professor of adult education and chair of the Department of Education, College of Agriculture and Life Sciences, Cornell University.*

RONALD M. CERVERO *is a professor of adult education, past head of the Department of Adult Education/Lifelong Education, Administration, and Policy, and associate dean of outreach and engagement in the College of Education, University of Georgia.*

New Directions for Adult and Continuing Education • DOI: 10.1002/ace

9

In the final chapter, the author reflects on some of the insights gained by the editors over these past months as they discussed the struggle for democracy and shared governance in the many spaces they refer to as adult education.

"Blues Is Easy to Play But Hard to Feel" (Jimi Hendrix)

Wendy Yanow

Understanding democracy reminds me a little bit of learning to play the guitar. It's pretty simple. If you know three chords you can play almost any rock and roll, blues, or folk song. You can write a soulful ballad about protest and workers' rights. You can write a love song and play it on YouTube for millions of viewers—even fancy yourself the next new "idol." But when Jimmy Hendrix played "Voodoo Child" it was anything but simple, and though millions of young musicians did and still do their best to copy that riff, nobody got to that gut-wrenching place where we both understood the world in all its complexities and at the same time could not find one word to describe it. My old guitar teacher used to call that kind of experience "other-worldly."

In this country, democracy seems a little "other-worldly," well, maybe more accurately and simply, fundamentally misunderstood. Americans commonly refer to our form of government as a democracy. And when it is in our interest, we feel compelled to insist that other nations implement some version of our form of democracy. But how many of us understand that rather than a pure democracy, where all citizens enjoy equal input, our form of government is a republic or a representative democracy in which a small subset of representatives create the laws by which we all must live? Although we continue to seek, often with some sincerity, pure democratic practices within our republic, we are, in fact, not a pure democracy. Perhaps it is as Hendrix said, "easy to play, but hard to feel."

Many Americans simply conflate democracy with capitalism, and then conflate capitalism with that notion referred to as the "American Dream." Were we a pure democracy, the recent healthcare debate would have been one in which the interests of those most affected—Americans without

New Directions for Adult and Continuing Education, no. 128, Winter 2010 © 2010 Wiley Periodicals, Inc.
Published online in Wiley Online Library (wileyonlinelibrary.com) • DOI: 10.1002/ace.394

healthcare coverage—would have had the loudest voices. Instead, those Americans fighting for their version of the "American Dream," that is, being able to keep the high-cost coverage that they worked hard to get, and to which they feel entitled, did so at the expense of those without coverage whose voices were often not heard. And when those opponents to healthcare reform lost their fight, they insisted that their democratic freedoms had been hoodwinked. Democracy, to those Americans, seemed to mean little more than individual freedom and rights.

In some ways, the practice of democracy is dialectically opposed to the practices of a republic. That one insists on a process where the voices of those least likely to be heard, farthest from the locus of control and power must be represented opposes, often dramatically, the notion that with representation those voices will be heard. And it is difficult to challenge the aspects of capitalism that get in the way of that kind of inclusive decision making when capitalism, as a free market economic system, has become synonymous with democracy, a political decision-making system. Hart reminded us of the enormity of this misunderstanding in Chapter four when she presented that relationship as "life-destroying logic."

Equally troubling is the unrecognized complexity of our collective understanding of democracy or democratic practice as a nation. In the United States there is such incredible complacency about both the meaning of democracy and our position as the great democratic nation that there is very little, if any, public debate on what is meant by democracy and what responsibilities we bear as a democratic nation. It is reminiscent of the ways in which racism, since the passage of civil rights and the rise of colorblindness as our dominant ideology on race, has become somewhat of a nonissue. We not only do not demand thoughtful or critical debate over the meaning of either of these concepts, we are offended when the suggestion surfaces that we are, in fact, a nation struggling with a history of racism, the foundations of which continue to plague our democratic process. Moreover, if we define democracy in some way beyond a simple majority rule, we might be mimicked as Harvard elitists who are too distant for regular folks to understand what is actually going on.

In response to the editors' growing recognition of the limits of our collective understanding of the substance of democracy, the focus of this text has included an exploration of the meaning of democracy and a drawing of the connection between democratic practice and adult education. At its core, one might conclude that the practice of democracy is the practice of adult education (Brookfield, 2010). That the process requires inclusive and thoughtful participation suggests a need for critical engagement. And critical engagement enacted through discussion suggests the presentation of multiple perspectives and supported arguments, the results of which often reflect a depth of understanding that can emerge from critical analysis of lived experience.

New Directions for Adult and Continuing Education • DOI: 10.1002/ace

Chapters of this issue demonstrate the breadth of adult education contexts within which some form of democratic practice is either an intentional organizational objective or an organic process in which people choose to learn and work together in an effort to effect collective good. Within some adult education graduate programs, there continues to be some interest in keeping that connection to our history alive. The requirement to engage in democratic practice within the National-Louis University doctoral adult education program, for example, is a reflection of a program whose philosophical roots reflect an understanding of education as a political process. The discord in that program appeared to have emerged as a result of both a lack of understanding and collective interest among the students in the messiness and complexity of engaging in a democratic process. Although there seemed to be individual understanding of the complexity of democracy there was never recognition of the need for collective understanding. Intellectually students may have been situated in a sociopolitical context, but they often responded from an individualistic point of view. On the other hand, the "teachable moment" happened when the former students and their teacher decided to reflect on their experiences and employed a democratic process to do so (Ramdeholl, Giordani, Heaney, and Yanow, 2010).

Organic processes such as the Chicago community writing workshop, the dialogue between the teacher and students at National-Louis University, the adult literacy program in New York City, and the niñeras from Chicago who found space to validate themselves as humans and workers and in the process began to recognize how liberal ideology contributed to their invisibility, are all reflections of the radical learning potential of democratic practice (Gordon and Ramdeholl, 2010; Hart, 2010; Hurtig and Adams, 2010; Ramdeholl, Giordani, Heaney, and Yanow, 2010). At the same time, these examples demonstrate that an essential component of both the democratic process and our ability to learn from it is the willingness to explore and critically analyze life experience including our experiences with power and privilege. Although almost fashionable today, it isn't enough to simply recognize when we hold power and privilege (Colin and Lund, 2010). To understand what that means to others and us requires an exploration of lifelong assumptions and beliefs in juxtaposition to others' assumptions. There is little more powerful than the point and counterpoint of a story, and a counter-story (Yanow, 2007).

As for the not-so-organic processes, such as those in which democracy was imposed upon the group, like the self-governance requirement in the doctoral program, or the requirement to employ a shared governance process in the administration of institutions of higher learning, in addition to being less effective, speak to the unrecognized complexity and lack of trust in others to make decisions in their own best interest. Even the administrators who used the metaphor of "working the planning table" when referring to program planning and recognizing power disparities, found it difficult to follow through on those ideas in addressing salary decisions. There have also been attempts to introduce democracy into the workplace, with varying degrees of success (Heaney, 2010; Jurmo, 2010; Ramdeholl, Giordani, Heaney, and Yanow, 2010; Wilson and Cervero, 2010).

Throughout these explorations, as the editors and authors of this issue we have considered the successes and challenges we face as we work to both understand and infuse democratic practice as both a philosophical point of view and a means to defining our work as teachers, administrators, researchers, and activists. We have reminded ourselves of the enormous potential democratic process has for shifting the tides of inequality and because of that potential, just how difficult it is to employ. And in comparing the organic to the inorganic approaches to democracy, the text serves as a commentary on where adult education began, as a movement, a vehicle for social change, and where it seems to reside most solidly today, as a reflection of a conservative society focused upon individual freedom, rights, and wealth. We are reminded that education exists in a sociocultural, political, and economic context and that our organizations and programs operate within the constraints of those contexts. That time has become accepted as an asset valued more highly than participation of all stakeholders is a testament to the ways in which our decision-making processes have been both objectified and commodified.

Organizational structure today speaks to efficiency and effectiveness. The simpler and more streamlined the process, the better. In some contexts that kind of process makes sense. But in the important decisions that reflect one's ability to engage in the broader sociocultural, political, and economic structures, efficiency is not necessarily going to help us dislodge power structures that keep some from engaging in the process while deeming others as the lifelong decision makers. By its very history, adult education has a responsibility to keep the struggle going. It's not enough to impose an intellectual academic process of self-governance on our programs. If we hope to realize democratic learning in any place other than a community-based, organically grown democratic process, we need to prepare ourselves to engage in the messiness of teaching about democracy. That process begins with an honest exploration of our life experience and how it *feels* to either be on the inside holding tightly or on the outside and reaching.

References

Brookfield, S. "Leading Democratically." In D. Ramdeholl, T. Giordani, T. Heany, and W. Yanow (eds.), *The Struggle for Democracy in Adult Education.* New Directions for Adult and Continuing Education, no. 128 (pp. 5–13). San Francisco: Jossey-Bass, 2010.

Colin, S.A.J., III, and Lund, C. L. "The Intersections of White Privilege and Racism: Moving Forward." In C. L. Lund and S.A.J. Colin (eds.), *White Privilege and Racism:*

Perceptions and Action. New Directions for Adult and Continuing Education, no. 125 (pp. 91–94). San Francisco: Jossey-Bass, 2010.

Gordon, J., and Ramdeholl, D. "'Everybody Had a Piece . . .' Collaborative Practice and Shared Decision Making at the Open Book." In D. Ramdeholl, T. Giordani, T. Heany, and W. Yanow (eds.), *The Struggle for Democracy in Adult Education.* New Directions for Adult and Continuing Education, no. 128 (pp. 27–35). San Francisco: Jossey-Bass, 2010.

Hart, M. "Radically Democratic Learning in the Grounded In-Between." In D. Ramdeholl, T. Giordani, T. Heany, and W. Yanow (eds.), *The Struggle for Democracy in Adult Education.* New Directions for Adult and Continuing Education, no. 128 (pp. 37–45). San Francisco: Jossey-Bass, 2010.

Heaney, T. "Democracy, Shared Governance, and the University." In D. Ramdeholl, T. Giordani, T. Heany, and W. Yanow (eds.), *The Struggle for Democracy in Adult Education.* New Directions for Adult and Continuing Education, no. 128 (pp. 69–79). San Francisco: Jossey-Bass, 2010.

Hurtig, J., and Adams, H. "Democracy Is in the Details: Small Writing Groups Prefiguring a New Society. In D. Ramdeholl, T. Giordani, T. Heany, and W. Yanow (eds.), *The Struggle for Democracy in Adult Education.* New Directions for Adult and Continuing Education, no. 128 (pp. 15–25). San Francisco: Jossey-Bass, 2010.

Jurmo, P. Productive and Participatory: Basic Education for High Performing and Actively Engaged Workers. In D. Ramdeholl, T. Giordani, T. Heany, and W. Yanow (eds.), *The Struggle for Democracy in Adult Education.* New Directions for Adult and Continuing Education, no. 128 (pp. 47–57). San Francisco: Jossey-Bass, 2010.

Ramdeholl, D., Giordani, T., Heaney, T., and Yanow, W. "Race, Power, and Democracy in the Graduate Classroom." In D. Ramdeholl, T. Giordani, T. Heany, and W. Yanow (eds.), *The Struggle for Democracy in Adult Education.* New Directions for Adult and Continuing Education, no. 128 (pp. 59–68). San Francisco: Jossey-Bass, 2010.

Wilson, A. L., and Cervero, R. M. "Democracy and Program Planning." In D. Ramdeholl, T. Giordani, T. Heany, and W. Yanow (eds.), *The Struggle for Democracy in Adult Education.* New Directions for Adult and Continuing Education, no. 128 (pp. 81–89). San Francisco: Jossey-Bass, 2010.

Yanow, W. B. *Autobiography as Counter-Narrative: An Empirical Study of How Race Enters and Structures the Stories of Our Lives.* Chicago: National-Louis University, 2007.

WENDY YANOW *is adjunct faculty at DePaul University, School for New Learning, Chicago and National-Louis University, College of Arts and Sciences, Chicago and a consultant in adult education.*

INDEX

recognizing their privilege, critiquing the impact on peoples of color, and making the decision to reconfigure their attitudes and alter their behaviors. This volume focuses on facilitating our understanding of the conceptual correlation between white privilege and racism and how these intertwined threads are manifested in selected areas of adult and continuing education practice. Although there seems to be a consensus that this practice reflects sociocultural and intellectual racism, there has been no discussion of linkages between the white racist ideology, white privilege, and white attitudes and behaviors behind that racism.
ISBN: 978-0-4706-3162-1

ACE124   Reaching Out Across the Border: Canadian Perspectives in Adult Education

Patricia Cranton, Leona M. English

This volume brings together Canadian scholars and practitioners to articulate a variety of historical, geographical, and political positions on the field of adult education in Canada. The chapter authors examine the country's interests and discourses and detail Canada's history, educational initiatives, movements, and linguistic struggles. Specifically, the authors address the uniqueness of Canada's emphasis on linking health and adult literacy; the use of video and dialogue to promote adult and literacy education in the North; the historical adult education initiatives such as Frontier College and the Antigonish movement; the special language and cultural issues that define Quebec's role of adult education and training; the development of critical adult education discourse in Canada; the emphasis on environmental adult education; the uniqueness of the community college system; and initiatives in adult education for community development. By describing Canadian accomplishments and lessons learned in adult education, this volume will help inform the practice, research, and studies of adult educators in the United States.
ISBN: 978-0-4705-9259-5

ACE123   Negotiating Ethical Practice in Adult Education

Elizabeth J. Burge

Here is a collection for twenty-first-century challenges! One practical philosopher and seven experienced adult educators dig into their driving values, the existing literature, and frank narratives of direct experience to illuminate key lessons in being one's own applied ethicist. In explaining their decision-making and confronting their unease and doubts, the authors emerge as self-aware, context-aware, principled practitioners. But they are not immune to the problems encountered in the intellectual and interpersonal complexities of ethical analysis.

Acknowledging the challenges in moving beyond such reductionist analyses as "right versus wrong," the authors look for negotiated possibilities of "rightness." Negotiation, reflection, and power emerge as three key themes of the reflective chapters. As a reader, you might consider the various thinking strategies offered, in particular the strategy of "sinning bravely." Additional critical thinking about conflicts that hide in the background of our work ought to help unearth some hegemonic uses of concepts such as fairness and justice.

Feel encouraged, feel strong, feel connected as you compare your own issues and thinking with the authors' experience and guidance. The reading journey of this issue of *New Directions for Adult and Continuing Education* will bring you closer to possibilities for more good work in the tough conditions of twenty-first-century adult education. ISBN: 978-0-4705-3971-2

ACE122 **Social Capital and Women's Support Systems: Networking, Learning, and Surviving**
Carmela R. Nanton, Mary V. Alfred
The concept of social capital goes back to the early twentieth century. Although it has sociological underpinnings, it has been primarily applied in the business arena. Increasingly, over the last two decades, there has been a proliferation of literature that proposes a broader application of the social capital concepts to individuals, communities, societies, and even adult learning.

This monograph applies social capital concepts to women as adult learners in learning communities, as users of technology, and as workers, and then integrates it from the perspective of adult education. We make the case that, because women tend to be more relational than men, their lives as students are integrally related to the social networks of which they are a part. We recognize that there are certain risks inherent in social capital networks and that gender bias can lead to exclusionary challenges that marginalize women as a group. On that basis, some feminist theorists have suggested that we simply eliminate the idea of social capital because of the inherent bias in the theory's underlying concepts and assumptions. Instead, we propose an integrationist approach that recognizes the relational nature of women, their historical and contemporary use of social capital networks, and the way they leverage such relationships for personal and community transformation.
ISBN: 978-0-4705-3734-3

ACE 121 **Bringing Community to the Adult ESL Classroom**
Clarena Larrotta, Ann K. Brooks
Using the concept of community building as a framework, this volume summarizes and updates readers on the state of adult English as a second language (ESL) education in the United States. It provides a complete description of this population of learners and their learning needs. The various chapters discuss possibilities for community building in the adult ESL classroom, combining research, theory, and practice. Community building is not a new topic; we often discuss it informally with our colleagues and students. However, scant written material exists—with a focus on adult ESL—documenting how it happens or reconciling theory with practitioners' experiences. In this volume, several practitioners and researchers explain the ways in which they use community-building principles in adult ESL settings. The authors' descriptions of applications of community-building principles can help other adult educators implement these ideas in their teaching practice. Our goal is to encourage readers to spark conversation and continuous learning among all who work in this field.
ISBN: 978-0-4704-7955-1

ACE120 **Adult Learning and the Emotional Self**
John M. Dirkx
Emotion is a pervasive force in adult learning—from fear, anxiety, dread, shame, and doubt to hope, excitement, joy, desire, and pride. For the most part, however, practitioners and scholars view the adult learning process as conceptual, rational, and cognitive. If emotion is

considered positively, it is as a helpful adjunct to the learning process. More often, it is regarded as a potential barrier that has to be worked through if effective learning is to occur. Although we are only beginning to attend to the powerful role that emotion can play in our lives as teachers and adult learners, a small but growing body of interdisciplinary scholarship provides an opportunity to revisit our earlier assumptions. This volume seeks to build on this emerging scholarship by focusing on the emotional self across a range of adult learning settings: basic and higher education, workplace learning, and formal and informal contexts. The chapters demonstrate, in different ways, the growing integration of emotion into more holistic, constructive ways of learning and knowing. As we attune to the emotional atmosphere in which we work, we stand a better chance of helping adult students achieve their educational goals—and we become better educators in the process. ISBN: 978-0-4704-4674-4

ACE119 Third Update on Adult Learning Theory

Sharan B. Merriam

This *Third Update on Adult Learning Theory* follows two earlier volumes on the same topic, the first published in 1993 and the second in 2001. Only one topic, transformative learning theory, can be found in all three updates, representing the continuing developments in research and alternative theoretical conceptions of TL. Thanks to a growing body of research and theory-building, three topics briefly touched on in 2001 are now separate chapters in this third update. They are on spirituality and adult learning, learning through the body, and narrative learning in adulthood. Also new in this update is a chapter on non-Western perspectives on learning and knowing. New developments in two other areas are also explored: understanding the connection between the brain and learning, and how modern and postmodern ways of knowing are converging and are being expressed in social movements. The concluding chapter identifies two trends in adult learning theory for the twenty-first century: attention to context, and to the holistic nature of learning in adulthood. ISBN: 978-0-4704-1785-0

ACE118 Linking Adults with Community: Promoting Civic Engagement through Community Based Learning

Susan C. Reed, Catherine Marienau

Adults are increasingly called upon to become involved in the body politic in order to strengthen their communities, promote change, and enliven our democracy. Competing with the call for civic engagement are the demanding priorities of modern life that adults face in the workplace, at home, and in their community. In community-based learning, universities partner with local organizations and nonprofits to provide experiences that promote the growth and development of both students and community residents. Careful project design is crucial to the accomplishment of these laudable outcomes. Employing community-based learning with adults presents unique challenges and opportunities; it requires an analysis of the adult-learning literature as well as identification of service-learning practices that will be effective with adults. In this volume, drawing upon adult-learning and service-learning literature and case studies, scholars and practitioners articulate best practices in community-based adult learning and illustrate its implementation. ISBN: 978-0-4703-8531-9

NEW DIRECTIONS FOR ADULT AND CONTINUING EDUCATION

ORDER FORM SUBSCRIPTION AND SINGLE ISSUES

DISCOUNTED BACK ISSUES:

Use this form to receive 20% off all back issues of *New Directions for Adult and Continuing Education*.
All single issues priced at **$23.20** (normally $29.00)

TITLE	ISSUE NO.	ISBN

Call 888-378-2537 or see mailing instructions below. When calling, mention the promotional code JBNND to receive your discount. For a complete list of issues, please visit www.josseybass.com/go/ndace

SUBSCRIPTIONS: (1 YEAR, 4 ISSUES)

☐ New Order   ☐ Renewal

U.S.	☐ Individual: $89	☐ Institutional: $259
CANADA/MEXICO	☐ Individual: $89	☐ Institutional: $299
ALL OTHERS	☐ Individual: $113	☐ Institutional: $333

Call 888-378-2537 or see mailing and pricing instructions below.
Online subscriptions are available at www.onlinelibrary.wiley.com

ORDER TOTALS:

Issue / Subscription Amount: $ _____

Shipping Amount: $ _____
(for single issues only – subscription prices include shipping)

Total Amount: $ _____

SHIPPING CHARGES:

First Item	$5.00
Each Add'l Item	$3.00

(No sales tax for U.S. subscriptions. Canadian residents, add GST for subscription orders. Individual rate subscriptions must be paid by personal check or credit card. Individual rate subscriptions may not be resold as library copies.)

BILLING & SHIPPING INFORMATION:

☐ **PAYMENT ENCLOSED:** *(U.S. check or money order only. All payments must be in U.S. dollars.)*

☐ **CREDIT CARD:**   ☐ VISA   ☐ MC   ☐ AMEX

Card number _____Exp. Date_____

Card Holder Name_____Card Issue # _____

Signature _____Day Phone_____

☐ **BILL ME:** *(U.S. institutional orders only. Purchase order required.)*

Purchase order # _____
Federal Tax ID 13559302 • GST 89102-8052

Name_____

Address_____

Phone_____ E-mail_____

Copy or detach page and send to: **John Wiley & Sons, PTSC, 5th Floor**
989 Market Street, San Francisco, CA 94103-1741

Order Form can also be faxed to: **888-481-2665**

PROMO JBNND

Statement of Ownership

Statement of Ownership, Management, and Circulation (required by 39 U.S.C. 3685), filed on OCTOBER 1, 2010 for NEW DIRECTIONS FOR ADULT AND CONTINUING EDUCATION (Publication No. 1058-2891), published Quarterly at Wiley Subscription Services, Inc. at Jossey-Bass, 989 Market St., San Francisco, CA 94103.

The names and complete mailing addresses of the Publisher, Editor, and Managing Editor are: Publisher, Wiley Subscription Services Inc., A Wiley Company at San Francisco, 989 Market St., San Francisco, CA 94103-1741; Editor, Coeditor Susan Imel, Ohio State University/Eric-Acve, 1900 Kenny Road, Columbus, OH 43210-1090; Managing Editor, Coeditor, Jovita M. Ross-Gordon, Texas State University, EAPS Department, 601 University Drive, San Marcos, TX 78666.

NEW DIRECTIONS FOR ADULT AND CONTINUING EDUCATION is a publication owned by Wiley Subscription Services, Inc. The known bondholders, mortgagees, and other security holders owning or holding 1% or more of total amount of bonds, mortgages, or other securities are (see list).

	Average No. Copies Each Issue During Preceding 12 Months	No. Copies Of Single Issue Published Nearest To Filing Date (Summer 2010)
15a. Total number of copies (net press run)	1,031	906
15b. Legitimate paid and/or requested distribution (by mail and outside mail)		
15b(1). Individual paid/requested mail subscriptions stated on PS form 3541 (include direct written request from recipient, telemarketing, and Internet requests from recipient, paid subscriptions including nominal rate subscriptions, advertiser's proof copies, and exchange copies)	336	307
15b(2). Copies requested by employers for distribution to employees by name or position, stated on PS form 3541	0	0
15b(3). Sales through dealers and carriers, street vendors, counter sales, and other paid or requested distribution outside USPS	0	0
15b(4). Requested copies distributed by other mail classes through USPS	0	0
15c. Total paid and/or requested circulation (sum of 15b(1), (2), (3), and (4))	336	307
15d. Nonrequested distribution (by mail and outside mail)		
15d(1). Outside county nonrequested copies stated on PS form 3541	29	29
15d(2). In-county nonrequested copies stated on PS form 3541	0	0
15d(3). Nonrequested copies distributed through the USPS by other classes of mail	0	0
15d(4). Nonrequested copies distributed outside the mail	0	0
15e. Total nonrequested distribution (sum of 15d(1), (2), (3), and (4))	29	29
15f. Total distribution (sum of 15c and 15e)	365	336
15g. Copies not distributed	666	570
15h. Total (sum of 15f and 15g)	1,031	906
15i. Percent paid and/or requested circulation (15c divided by 15f times 100)	92.4%	91.3%

I certify that all information furnished on this form is true and complete. I understand that anyone who furnishes false or misleading information on this form or who omits material or information requested on this form may be subject to criminal sanctions (including fines and imprisonment) and/or civil sanctions (including civil penalties).

(signed) Susan E. Lewis, VP & Publisher-Periodicals